Curriculum innovation

Curriculum innovation

A celebration of classroom practice

Roger Crombie White

Open University Press
Buckingham • Philadelphia

Open University Press
Celtic Court
22 Ballmoor
Buckingham
MK18 1XW

and

1900 Frost Road, Suite 101
Bristol, PA 19007, USA

First published 1997

A catalogue record of this book is available from the British Library

ISBN   0 335 19767 4 (hbk)   0 335 19756 6 (pbk)

Library of Congress Cataloging-in-Publication Data
White, Roger Crombie, 1949–
    Curriculum innovation : a celebration of classroom practice /
Roger Crombie White.
        p.   cm.
    Includes bibliographical references and index.
    ISBN 0–335–19767–4. — ISBN 0–335–19756–6 (pbk.)
    1. Education, Secondary—Great Britain—Curricula.   2. Curriculum
planning—Great Britain.   3. Teacher participation in curriculum
planning—Great Britain.   4. Curriculum change—Great Britain—Case
studies.   I. Title.
LB1629.5.G7W55   1997
373.19′0941—dc20
                                                        96-33217
                                                        CIP

Typeset by Graphicraft Typesetters Ltd., Hong Kong
Printed in Great Britain by St Edmundsbury Press Ltd,
Bury St Edmunds, Suffolk

To Chris

With love

Contents

Preface

In 1970 I took up my first post, teaching science and drama in a secondary school whose catchment area included the sons and daughters of the scientists who worked at the Atomic Weapons Research establishment near Aldermaston. Splitting atoms in the classroom was child's play for such a group. Despite parental pressure the head steadfastly refused to sanction O levels within the school. CSEs were the order of the day and the whole staff team were encouraged to write and submit Mode 3 versions for approval by the local CSE board.

As someone whose whole experience as a pupil in a direct grant grammar school had been defined by the pressures to perform well at GCE examinations, this concentration on CSEs seemed rather quirky. In my own case the conformity and uniformity and consequent predictability of O and A levels had been such that both teachers and pupils could legitimately spend hours in discussing what would 'come up in the exam'. The really clever pupils were those who had a good grasp of this probability analysis.

CSE Mode 3 offered no such possibilities. The course work requirements and the individualized nature of the examination made it impossible to engage in such prediction exercises. Far from limiting assessment to memory and recall, the whole structure of a Mode 3 CSE was designed to evaluate knowledge, understanding and the ability to solve problems – a veritable Pandora's box of Bloom's taxonomy of educational objectives.

Those were heady days indeed for a new recruit to the profession. Individual teachers had the power to design a course and its assessment framework, the responsibility for delivering the content in whatever way they chose and the opportunity to sharpen professional judgement about standards through discussion with other teachers at the regional moderation of candidates' work. Professional autonomy had a real ring to it then.

At the time I simply took it for granted that this was what teachers did. Classroom teaching was just one part of a collaborative process with other professionals that included curriculum and assessment design as an integral part of the job. Department meetings and staff meetings took these issues very seriously, and it was a common experience to sit in the staff room round the tea trolley after school and explore questions of course design.

Maybe I was lucky. It was 1970 and the comprehensive system was expanding and flourishing. There were some remarkable teachers in that school. Maurice Bound was the head and Alan Weaver the head of science. Other names are still strong in my memory although it's more than twenty years ago. I was infected by their professionalism. I believed that teachers could change things for the better, so much so that when I left the school near Aldermaston in the mid-1970s it was to work with an emerging project for disaffected adolescents in Bristol. This project, a development of the Youth Education Service charity, was experimenting with 'alternative' curriculum processes to break the cycle of failure and disillusionment that had been the common experience for all of them in school. Together with Dave Brockington, my friend from our time as undergraduates at York University, and an impressive team of people in Bristol, this project expanded to the point where its curriculum significance was recognized by the Schools Council, who approved and funded a national dissemination programme. This project and its successes (and failures) are well documented in *In and Out of School* (White and Brockington 1978).

One of the major outcomes of this project was the establishment of the Bayswater Centre, offering full-time education for 'disaffected' pupils in their final years of compulsory schooling. Funded by Avon LEA, this school was a teacher's dream. Those of us who were involved at the outset had a free hand in the design of the curriculum. We could do pretty much what we wanted, as long as we continued to demonstrate success in terms of attendance, appropriate behavioural change, examination achievement and subsequent employment or further education and training. Much of the inspiration for this work came from the writings of Illich, Reimer, Holt, Kohl, Freire, Neill and other authors published in the 'Penguin Education Special' series. One book that influenced me considerably was *State School* by R. F. Mackenzie (1970). In describing the series of residential trips that pupils from his secondary modern school in the Scottish coal fields made to a disused railway building on Rannoch Moor in the Highlands, Mackenzie inspired thousands of teachers (myself included) with his vision of learning.

> On a short week end a child may have the luck to watch a dragonfly emerge from its pupa in Lochaber or listen to the fluting notes of the golden plover on the high ground above Rannoch and store the memory against the dark days. But we want more than just these tantalising glimpses of a different world; we want to give pupils the chance of a deeper immersion in a different way of life, and longer enduring memories. There will be no compulsion, no pressure, no 'hurry up', no examinations. If they want to climb or ski we'll help them acquire the skills. If they want to identify alpine plants or birds, we'll see that the knowledge is available. And when they have no yearning for activity or thirst for knowledge but just want to sit, like the Highlanders who were here before them, and watch the cloud scudding over Creag Dhubh, or listen to

raindrops falling through the branches after the rain has stopped, that also is an important part of growth. It is in such times that half sub-merged fears, ideas, hopes, questions, float to the surface.

(Mackenzie 1970: 103)

That book and a visit made to an experimental *efterskole* in Denmark in 1978, which was demonstrating some impressive results with very 'difficult' adolescents, did more than anything else to inform my own approach to curriculum development, the rationale for which is described in *Absent with Cause* (White 1980). At the Bayswater Centre the team of staff took re-sponsibility for devising the curriculum – in consultation with the pupils and their parents. The *implementation* of many aspects of it was also a shared endeavour, as evidenced by a number of television programmes that featured the Bayswater Centre during this period (HTV 1980; Granada 1981; Thames 1983).

Soon after the inception of this school, HMI published *Curriculum 11–16* (HMI 1977b), which described the curriculum under 'areas of experience'. This document provided a powerful legitimacy for our own structure, which tended very much to focus on the young people's overall personal develop-ment, to which a whole range of experiences (*including* traditional subjects) made a significant contribution.

The publication of *Absent with Cause* coincided with a movement that was already gathering pace to celebrate and promote the excellent curriculum development of similar 'off-site' schools and units. The National Organisa-tion for Initiatives in Social Education (NOISE), with initial support from the Schools Curriculum Development Committee (SCDC), became the umbrella support group for a network of teachers, youth and community workers, social workers, probation officers and other professional groups who were active in this area of curriculum development. NOISE attracted some ener-getic people, like Howie Armstrong, Claudia Beamish, Jeff Crow, Pat Dain, Gethin Davies, Rod Ling, Nick Peacey, Marion Pearson, Delwyn Tattum, Rob Whitehouse and Ian Wilson, many of whom are still working at the sharp end of curriculum development in schools, colleges and youth centres.

It had an energetic run for ten years before fizzling out in the early 1990s. Bayswater Centre lasted rather longer, finally done to death after nearly twenty years by an LEA whose shortsighted and flawed reorganization plan for special education failed to recognize that a school with a national repu-tation for excellence might offer a local blueprint for successful practice. It was a remarkable demonstration of the principle of the 'prophet from within your own country' syndrome, with local jealousies appearing to play some part in the decisions. The LEA itself has since disappeared, and the new authorities it has spawned are now beginning to consider how to respond to the growing crisis of school exclusion. No doubt something like the Bayswater Centre will emerge again in due course, staffed by a new generation of energetic young teachers.

However, before their demise, both NOISE and the Bayswater Centre con-tributed to a fortuitous sequence of events and meetings that has resulted in one of the most remarkable curriculum development initiatives this century.

Impressed by a visit to the Bayswater Centre in 1980, Professor Richard Pring drew its work and that of the Youth Education Service to the attention of the members of a 14–18 curriculum working party which he chaired at Exeter University. The principal aim of this group was to share and spread 'good practice' among the participating schools and colleges. One of the members of this group, Brian Fletcher, as deputy head of a school in Exeter, had constructed his own internal 'award scheme' so as to offer accreditation to his fifth year group for a whole range of achievements that weren't being recognized within the traditional examination system. 'It's not a question of passing or failing; it's about rewarding success,' explained Brian, and the Schools Council dissemination programme, coordinated by the Youth Education Service, was able to offer £700 towards the construction of an award scheme base in his school.

The annual NOISE conferences offered Brian further opportunities to share his award scheme model with other professional groups. His workshops at the conferences were always oversubscribed, attracting teachers who were keen to hear about an example of curriculum innovation that clearly worked, and one which they could easily emulate.

TVEI started in Exeter in 1983 and Brian Fletcher was able to use its resources to promote the scheme as a curriculum opportunity for all fourth and fifth year pupils in the school. In 1985 he became head of Coombeshead School in Newton Abbot and, under the leadership of an energetic head of year, Rita Rose, the school became the driving force for developing the scheme within a regional consortium of local secondary schools. Television South West offered some sponsorship and the Award Scheme gained credibility with local employers. 'I only wish I could have done it when I was at school,' said one father, echoing the views of many parents.

On 18 October 1987 the BBC featured the scheme as the main item on the *Education Programme*, and the response it generated led to the setting up of regional consortia in Avon and Berkshire, in addition to the now thriving network in Devon.

These three consortia of teachers worked together as a loose-knit federation for two years to revise and rewrite the materials for national dissemination. In the spring of 1990 a series of regional conferences was staged in Taunton, York, Edinburgh, Liverpool and London to offer the scheme to interested teachers in other LEAs. By September 3000 young people were enrolled on the scheme. A year later this figure had grown to 5000. By 1993 it was 30,000 and in 1995 the number of registrations pushed past the 100,000 mark.

For me the wheel has turned full circle.

As I take part in the regional moderation of young people's work that characterizes the accreditation structure of this particular award scheme I am reminded of those heady days in the early 1970s at the school in Aldermaston, where CSE Mode 3s were the common experience. I observe teachers exercising professional judgement in a way that both highlights their creative imagination and demonstrates what this imagination can actually achieve. For ten years I have witnessed the remarkable expansion of the scheme, and marvelled at the way in which teachers have developed the original ideas, while sustaining and retaining the underpinning principle of rewarding achievement.

And all this has happened at a time when curriculum development has increasingly become centrally directed and controlled, with millions of pounds spent on glossy brochures and advertising from the government agencies responsible. In 1995 Oxfordshire LEA published a table illustrating just some of the extra costs associated with the implementation of the National Curriculum up until January 1994. The expenditure on National Curriculum documents alone came to £469 million.[1]

The operating costs of the Award Scheme Development and Accreditation Network (ASDAN), which benefits more than 120,000 young people in several thousand schools and colleges, have yet to top half a million a year.

This book is intended to be a celebration of the whole notion of teacher-led curriculum development at the secondary level of schooling, with the ASDAN Award Scheme offered as a particular 'case study' in Chapter 8. Its overriding intention is to draw attention to the creative talent within the profession, and demonstrate some of the ways this is being translated into classroom practice throughout the country, despite pressures to centralize control of curriculum development.

The time is right for such celebration. It is very necessary to provide a counterbalance to the prevailing view (largely media inspired and not necessarily accurate) that teachers are suffering from 'low morale'. The history of teachers as curriculum innovators is rich and inspirational. The introduction of GCSEs and the national curriculum may have cast a cloud over the capacity of the profession to initiate original development work itself. That cloud is lifting though, as politicians in particular and policy makers in general begin to recognize the weaknesses of the 1988 Act and subsequent legislation.

As the pendulum begins to swing back from the centrally controlled and narrowly prescriptive programmes of study and attainment targets of the National Curriculum, it is important to highlight areas of good practice and identify the policy implications of these grass roots initiatives.

NOTE

1 The Oxfordshire list itemized the following: £469 million on national curriculum documents and SATs; £8.7 million spent by the DfE publicity to schools; £3.0 million spent on the Parents' Charter; £2.0 million on the Dearing 'consultation' on the National Curriculum; £36.3 million on the National Curriculum Council (NCC) operating costs; £69.6 million on the Schools Examination and Assessment Council (SEAC) operating costs; £2.0 million on producing secondary school league tables each year; £100 million on school inspections by Ofsted.

Acknowledgements

This book owes its emergence to a great many people.

All my former colleagues at the Hurst Comprehensive School who triggered my commitment to teaching.

Those many colleagues in the University of the West of England (UWE) Faculty of Education (including Gay Attwood, Gill Blunden, David James, Don Kimber, Ian Menter, Mike Nicholson and Lynn Raphael Reed) who have offered feedback and inspiration and support at various stages in the writing of this.

Judith Stewart, the Subject Librarian at Redland Campus, University of the West of England, for her painstaking research, advice and wonderful sense of humour as we trawled through the mountains of literature on curriculum issues.

Ed Morris, from Den Frie Laeverskole in Denmark, for his help in researching data on Danish society for Chapters 3 and 4.

Brian Fletcher and Peter Gallie for the detailed curriculum maps of their respective schools, which illuminate Chapter 5.

Chris Drower, the Administrative Co-ordinator of the ASDAN Award Scheme, for the distribution, collection and collation of the questionnaire data that form the substantive part of Chapters 7 and 8.

The 190 respondents to the questionnaire in schools and colleges around the UK (whose names are listed in the Appendix).

The 1830 teachers and lecturers who currently coordinate the ASDAN Award Scheme in the participating schools and colleges throughout the UK, the thousands more colleagues in those same institutions who support them in this work and all the teachers who worked together in the various LEAs in the early years of the award scheme to develop the materials and establish the first consortia groups on which these subsequent developments have been able to build.

The team of 42 regional coordinators and area coordinators (Carolyn Baines, Clive Baker, Tim Bancroft, Liz Bass, Dave Bastow, John Bell, Mark Betts,

Edna Beveridge, Phil Braide, Pat Brennan, Sue Burge, Linda Chance, Caroline Corkrum, Pat Cowan, Mike Creary, Anna Crispin, Heather Fry, Di Fuller, Angela Gibson, Clare Grandi, Kath Grant, Marie Gray, Rennie Halstead, Trevor Harden, Bob Harding, Sylvia Holt, Michele Humphreys, Ian Hutchinson, Marilyn Jones-Hill, Carol Jordon, Jane Joyce, Steve Kraemer, Nick Lewis, Graham Lloyd, Elva Longfoot, Lynn McCann, Fiona Miller, Terry Monks, Mary Moore, Wyn Morgan, Mike Niblett, Viv Nicholls, Eddie Parker, Lesley Preece, Mark Reader, George Richardson, Rita Rose, Anthony Sampson, Hazel Saunders, Janet Schofield, Julie Stevenson, Lut Stewart, Susan Straw, Elaine Swales, Brenda Thornton, Jane Williams, Diane Wraight and Sara Young) who maintain the ASDAN consortium network around the UK.

The coordinating committee for the ASDAN Award Scheme (Dave Brockington, Chris Drower, Trisha Fettes, Brian Fletcher, Steve Harper, Brian Hobbs, Rita Rose, and Karen Swaffield) for managing its development over the past ten years.

The team of people in the ASDAN central office (Ann Boote, Annette Cornish, Abby Doig, Barlie Doig, Chris Drower, Clive Irons, Sally Murphy, Tara Perry, Dot Sealey, Theresa Spiring, Mary Tarling and Lesley Wyrill) who maintain the administrative heart of the organization.

Shona Mullen for catalysing the germination of this book, and for her constructive comments that helped to shape the final draft of the manuscript.

And all those friends, writers and practitioners whose experiences, thoughts and ideas about educational issues have inspired me since I first started teaching 27 years ago.

List of abbreviations

A level	Advanced level
AS level	Advanced Supplementary level
ASDAN	Award Scheme Development and Accreditation Network
AUT	Association of University Teachers
BTEC	Business and Technician Education Council
CBI	Confederation of British Industry
CGLI	City of Guilds of London Institute
CPVE	Certificate of Pre-Vocational Education
CSE	Certificate of Secondary Education
CTC	City Technology College
DES	Department of Education and Science
DfE	Department for Education
DfEE	Department for Education and Employment
DoE/ED	Department of Employment/Employment Department
DOVE	Diploma of Vocational Education
ERASMUS	European Community Action Scheme for the Mobility of University Students
EU	European Union
FE	further education
FEFC	Further Education Funding Council
FEU	Further Education Unit
GCE	General Certificate of Education
GCSE	General Certificate of Secondary Education
GNVQ	General National Vocational Qualification
HE	higher education
HMI	Her Majesty's Inspectorate
HMSO	Her Majesty's Stationery Office
INSET	in-service training
IPPR	Institute of Public Policy Research
IT	information technology

LEA   local education authority
LEATG   local education authority training grant
LIB   lead industry body
LMS   local management of schools
MSC   Manpower Services Commission
NCC   National Curriculum Council
NCVQ   National Council for Vocational Qualifications
NFER   National Foundation for Educational Research
NISER   National Institute of Social and Economic Research
NOISE   National Organisation for Initiatives in Social Education
NRA   National Record of Achievement
NROVA   National Record of Vocational Achievement
NTET   National Training and Education Target
NVQ   National Vocational Qualification
OECD   Organisation for Economic Co-operation and Development
Ofsted   Office for Standards in Education
PGCE   Post Graduate Certificate in Education
PSE   personal and social education
ROA   Records of Achievement
RSA   Royal Society of Arts
SCAA   School Curriculum and Assessment Authority
SCOTVEC   Scottish Vocational Educational Council
SEAC   Secondary Examinations and Assessment Council
SEN   special educational needs
S/NVQ   Scottish National Vocational Qualification
TEC   Training and Enterprise Council
TEMPUS   Trans European Mobility Programme for University Students
TES   *Times Educational Supplement*
TUC   Trades Union Congress
TVEI   Technical and Vocational Education Initiative
UCAS   Universities and Colleges Admission Service
UWE   University of the West of England
YAS   Youth Award Scheme
YDP   Youth Development Programme
YT   Youth Training

Introduction

On 15 March 1996 the *Times Educational Supplement* (hereafter *TES*) published a letter by Mike Newby in which he took issue with many of the publications produced by educational researchers:

> It is lamentable that university specialists in educational thought and policy seem to perpetuate the very fog they are supposed to be most able to dispel, being versed in critical reflection, and possessing sharpness of insight and clarity of vision. Few academics write or speak in a style that is both understandable and highly relevant to a wide public... they pour all their efforts into churning out obscure articles for irrelevant journals which are only read by those who have to churn out obscure articles to aid the all-important research rating of the hand that feeds them. Academic research and reflection in education has largely become an esoteric world of interest only to itself (with notable exceptions).
>
> (Newby 1996)

Mike Newby's words echoed those of Professor Richard Pring, Director of Oxford University Department of Educational Studies, whose editorial for the summer 1995 edition of the *British Journal of Education* drew attention to the consequences of the Research Assessment Exercise – the four-yearly cycle by which universities are graded and funded accordingly.

> Has the frenzied attempt to produce more books, more articles, more reports, necessarily brought an improvement in educational literature? Has the emphasis upon *more* research in *every* institution encouraged *better* research? Are we now better informed, or is policy carried out more intelligently, as a result of the multi-fold increase in investigations? Do schools feel that they are benefiting from all the theoretical work about schools? And is teaching the beneficiary or the victim of the disaggregation of the funding of research from the funding of teaching?
>
> (Pring 1995b)

Professor David Hargreaves made a similar point the following year in urging teachers, academics, parents and governors to establish a new forum to decide what research should actually be carried out. In his view the £50–60 million spent every year on educational research gave poor value for money and was seen as irrelevant by most teachers. Much current educational research was second rate and 'cluttered up academic journals that virtually nobody reads' (Whitehead 1996).

Mike Newby, Richard Pring and David Hargreaves are making a serious charge against the world of educational 'academia' – a charge that finds popular support among many teachers who rubbish the value of 'theory', who rarely pick up scholarly texts for bedside reading and can find nothing in the outpourings from university faculties of education that affects their practice.

This is unfortunate, as there are sufficient 'notable exceptions' of the kind referred to by Mike Newby that deserve a wide audience. Some of this research influences the *policy* that shapes subsequent practice, as Professor Patricia Broadfoot made clear in a letter to the *TES* defending the quality of the National Evaluation of Records of Achievement.

> When the results of the evaluation were published in the late 1980s, there was enormous interest from teachers, LEA personnel, school governors, parents and the media, as well as academics ... The records of achievement initiative represented what was arguably a unique partnership between government, teachers, Her Majesty's Inspectorate and researchers. Teacher enthusiasm fuelled the Government's policy initiative, Teachers and researchers together provided the evidence which informed the 1989 guidelines ... The national record of achievement is now an entitlement for every pupil.
>
> (Broadfoot 1996)

And some of this research influences *practice* directly, if only teachers can override the powerful effect of the myth that educational texts are not for them. This generally requires time and space though, two commodities which have been squeezed in recent years. It requires commitment from the top to ensure that those working at the chalkface are supported in this process of reflective analysis, in the way that Professor Tim Brighouse, Chief Education Officer for Birmingham, has demonstrated with his promotion of the writing and thinking of Howard Gardner in Birmingham schools (Brighouse 1994).

Although this book doesn't claim to be in the same league as Howard Gardner, it is also written for a wide audience. It is about successful classroom practice. It is a book *about* teachers for teachers and others with any interest in what is happening in UK classrooms, and I hope goes some way to addressing the criticisms levelled against 'academia' by Mike Newby. It is intended to provide a readable and informative basis for discussion about the issues surrounding curriculum innovation and teacher autonomy, as well as offering some examples of good practice.

In Chapters 1 and 2 I have attempted to set the whole issue of curriculum development and professional autonomy in some sort of historical and contemporary context. To do it justice I have drawn extensively from the writing and the research of others, and have included various quotations, from practitioners, researchers and policy makers, that seem to me further to illustrate important points. With the help of Judith Stewart, the Subject Librarian at the Redland Campus of the University of the West of England, I have trawled through hundreds of texts and articles on curriculum issues, so as to provide you with a reference point for what follows in subsequent chapters. The extensive list of books and articles quoted at the end of each of these chapters is there to enable you to pursue issues in more depth, if you so choose. Feel free to skip these chapters, if you find that such writing makes you reach for the light switch beside your bed.

Chapter 3 considers the whole issue of 'underpinning values'. What are the beliefs that drive particular policy and practice? What is the nature of the society that we want the education system to serve? For me, this chapter has some special significance, as I have a commitment to the exploration of such questions in my own work with student teachers, and those teachers with whom I work on the ASDAN Award Scheme. I appreciate that this enters contentious territory – considering 'controversial matters' that Lawrence Stenhouse used to talk about in relation to the much acclaimed Humanities Curriculum Project of the early 1970s – but it is an area that I believe no attempt to make sense of policy and practice can avoid.

Chapter 4 offers some international perspectives, against which developments in the UK can be measured. Increasingly, it seems, emphasis is being put on comparisons with our 'competitors' abroad. League tables of educational achievements are often used to suggest that our 'system' is underperforming, with all the attendant implications about the effectiveness of our schools and our teachers. Are such comparisons valid and fair?

Chapter 5 gives you the 'map of the territory' for current and projected 14–19 curriculum development, with case studies at the end of how the map has been translated into the curriculum structure in two schools. For many people this will be familiar ground. Practitioners in schools and colleges will be only too well aware of the initiative overload that has swamped the curriculum terrain with a slurry of acronyms. The attempt here is to provide a snapshot of what is currently on offer for the 14–19 age group throughout England and Wales. There are bound to be some omissions. A glance through the DfE list of courses which have 'Specific approval' (DfE 1995) reveals more than a thousand qualifications, and this list takes no account of the several thousand programmes that come under the heading of 'General approval'.

Chapter 6 considers examples of teachers as curriculum innovators and draws attention to the tremendous number of school and college based initiatives that have resulted from professional enthusiasm and commitment. Such examples of 'good practice' have also been highlighted by the National Commission on Education in its report *Learning to Succeed* (1993).

Chapter 7 offers the views of teachers and lecturers in schools and colleges throughout the UK about curriculum innovation, the status of teachers and recent reforms. The comments here might well strike a chord with you as you find the observations mirror your own experience of education over the past few decades. The oldest teacher here has 34 years' experience with young people, the youngest 18 months'. Between the two ends of the continuum there are thousands of years of classroom contact encapsulated in the direct comments of the 190 professionals who responded to the survey that went out to 1700 secondary and tertiary establishments.

Chapter 8 describes the most impressive example of teacher-led curriculum development that has taken place this century. Not only does the ASDAN Award Scheme provide a curriculum enrichment programme for teachers and lecturers that embraces much of what is cherished under the heading of personal and social education (PSE), but it offers a way of accrediting it as well. It makes sense of the emerging emphasis on 'key skills' by helping students and teachers to gather evidence of attainment through settings that provide contextualization for the knowledge gained and skills developed. In rewarding students' success through its stepped programme of challenges, it demonstrably increases motivation. It achieves all the curriculum aspirations expressed by HMI in *Better Schools* (1985). The evidence is clear, as teachers coming to the scheme for the first time listen to fellow professionals describing the sixth form 'enrichment' experience it offers for applicants to higher education, as well as the benefits for those with special educational needs.

Throughout these chapters, consideration is given to some ways forward. There have been a number of reports in recent years arguing for a more coherent structure for upper secondary and tertiary education and training. Some, like *Learning for the Future* (Richardson *et al.* 1995) and *14–19 Education and Training* (Crombie White *et al.* 1995), are more visionary and potentially more challenging for policy makers than the rather safe recommendations of the much heralded Dearing Report on post-16 provision. It is to be hoped that a new government will have the courage to take on board some of the vision.

What is clear from the experience that this book describes and reflects, of the teachers and lecturers around the UK who are involved with curriculum innovation such as the ASDAN Award Scheme, is that professional commitment is still high. This book is intended to be a celebration of this remarkable development and is dedicated to the thousands of practitioners who have worked together since the early 1980s to create a curriculum model which can truly claim to be 'broad, balance, relevant and differentiated' (HMI 1985).

The hope is that the inspiration of the practice described in this book will enthuse you, the reader, and will go some way towards enhancing the 'P' of professional autonomy.

one

History of curriculum control

'Who should decide what should be taught in school?' has been a hotly debated question for as long as schools have existed. It raises all sorts of other questions, of course, about the purpose of schooling, the kind of society we want, whether some knowledge is more important than other knowledge, whether all children should learn the same things and at what ages . . . and so on.

Those who started the first 'schools' weren't necessarily in agreement about the answers to these questions. Elizabethan grammar schools, Dame schools, church schools, Sunday schools, public schools, Lancastrian schools, mechanics institutes and philanthropic schools differed widely in their aims and aspirations, reflecting the different value systems of those who paid for them. Indeed, the origins of schooling in the UK have a tradition stretching back to a period long before state intervention (Lawson and Silver 1973; Sanderson 1983). It was only in the mid-nineteenth century that the government considered it appropriate to put aside money from the central exchequer for the funding of education. These were tiny amounts to begin with. In 1833, when Parliament approved the first annual grant of £20,000 for education, this sum was less than the money earmarked for the King's racehorses. By 1856, the year that saw the end of the Crimean War, which had cost the country £78 million, the annual parliamentary grant for education had risen to £251,000 (Adamson 1964).

However, as government funding for public education increased during Queen Victoria's reign, it was considered appropriate to legislate for some measure of central control over what was actually taught in schools. In arguing for the 'Revised Code' in 1862, Robert Lowe warned that:

> a state of things will arise that the control of the educational system will pass out of the hands of the Privy Council and of the House of Commons into the hands of persons working that education system.
>
> (Tropp 1957)

The code introduced a system of grants to schools which became known as 'payment by results'. Each school received a grant equivalent to 40 pence a year for every pupil who attended for more than 200 days. In addition, each pupil aged 7 or over was tested every year in reading, writing and arithmetic, and one-third of the grant was deducted for those who failed. Given the sums of money involved it is not surprising that the three Rs became a principal focus of concern for teachers. Nor is it surprising that enrolment of 3- and 4-year-olds mushroomed in the years after the code was introduced, as schools desperately tried to increase the percentage of 7-year-olds who could achieve the required standard.

Though payment by results was officially abolished in 1895, its legacy was longer lived. Central control of the elementary curriculum was not actually relaxed until 1926, and it took until 1944 for the same degree of autonomy to be extended to secondary schools. Some aspects of the code are still with us. The school year for the state system continues to require 200 days attendance (with a late twentieth-century allowance for INSET days), and the recent introductions of tests for 7-, 11- and 14-year-olds bear some resemblance in their consequences to what Charles Dickens was writing about the common schools in Victorian Britain:

> Now, what I want is Facts. Teach these boys and girls nothing but Facts. Facts alone are wanted in life. Plant nothing else, and root out everything else. You can only form the minds of reasoning animals upon Facts: nothing else will ever be of any service to them. This is the principle on which I bring up my own children and this is the principle on which I bring up these children. Stick to Facts, sir!
>
> (Thomas Gradgrind in *Hard Times*)

Those coming into the profession in the years since the 1988 Education Act could be forgiven for believing that is has been 'ever thus'. A centrally prescribed curriculum, and clear programmes of study, age-related attainment targets and a system of funding that is related to pupil numbers in schools (which are determined by the school's popularity with parents, and influenced in no small part by its standing in the 'league tables') are common features of the state system. And now we have the proposal from some quarters that performance at GCSEs and truancy statistics should be taken into account in determining the funding a school receives.

There is a strong sense of history repeating itself as parallels are drawn with 'payment by results'. Various writers (such as Lawton 1984, 1989, 1992; Skilbeck 1984; Whitty 1985; Pring 1989, 1995a; Dale *et al.* 1990; Tomlinson 1993) have analysed the shift towards a more centralized control of the curriculum since the Second World War, which culminated in the 1988 Act and the provision of a 'national curriculum' for the 5–16 age group.

However, prior to the 1988 Act there was a period of about thirty years in which the responsibility for curriculum issues lay largely with schools, teachers and LEAs. This period between the end of the Second World War and the mid-seventies is quite unusual in the history of curriculum control in the United Kingdom, and consideration of what went on during this time

1950's

offers some remarkable insights into the consequences of a more devolved approach to curriculum innovation and implementation.

The 1944 Act provided a form of secondary education as a right for all 11–15-year-olds and relaxed the stranglehold on the curriculum that central government had previously exercised. The Act underlined the famous notion of 'partnership', with local education authorities, central government, churches, employers, parents and teachers all considered to have a legitimate interest and role to play in the organization and management of schools. While LEAs organized and administered the schools, in practice it was left to individual heads and teachers to determine curriculum priorities (with the exception of religious education, which *had* to be taught). The curriculum was regarded as a professional matter to be left to those who had been appropriately trained. The public examination system (controlled in the main by universities) and parental expectations both set some substantial limits on this control, but teachers retained and exercised considerable 'professional autonomy' over what they taught in the classroom; so much so that when David Eccles, the Minister for Education, established his own Curriculum Study Group in 1962 to enquire into the content of the 'secret garden' of the curriculum, the hostility it provoked from the teaching profession and local authorities resulted in the Study Group being replaced in 1964 by a representative body called the Schools Council for Curriculum and Examinations, which had a majority of teachers on its management board.

This quango was charged with the responsibility of promoting, managing and monitoring curriculum development in schools, and reforming the examination system (Morrell 1966). Through its management group structure, the profession exercised considerable influence over every aspect of the school curriculum. As well as providing a vehicle for the dissemination of 'good practice' between and among schools and colleges, the Schools Council initiated and funded remarkable curriculum development programmes of its own. Some, like Lawrence Stenhouse's 'Humanities Curriculum Project' (Stenhouse 1967, 1975), 'The Science 5–13 Project' (Harlen 1973), or the 'Geography for the Young School Leaver' project (Walker 1979; Dalton 1988), quickly gained a national reputation for excellence. Alongside the expanding programme of comprehensivisation during the 1960s and 1970s, teachers were actively encouraged to take initiative for curriculum development, and the literature for this period is rich in accounts of such creative activity.

Around this time the introduction of the Certificate of Secondary Education (CSE), with its Mode 3 regulations, provided an opportunity for teachers to devise and examine their own syllabuses in subject areas of their own choosing. Individual teachers had the power to design the course and its assessment framework, the responsibility for delivering the content in whatever way they chose and the opportunity to sharpen 'professional judgement' through discourse with colleagues. Professional autonomy had a real ring to it then and, although research into Mode 3 CSEs has indicated that they were often perceived as of less worth than the more traditional O levels (Whitty 1983), there were some remarkable whole school responses to this opportunity that transformed the educational experience and sense of achievement of many students.

Young teachers blink in surprise at the accounts of what went on within the context of CSE Mode 3. It seems an alien concept these days to talk about teachers having total control of what to teach and how to teach it; or to talk of a time when individual teachers devised the assessment framework (which included large elements of course work), set and marked the final exam and moderated their overall assessments in discussion with teachers from other schools; and all this without interference from external agencies. It appears strange to contemplate how employers and further and higher education trusted these professional judgements about a course whose upper grading possessed the same currency as O levels. Yet this was the world that teachers inhabited 20 years ago.

What happened to change it all? How has the locus of control moved so dramatically from the schools and the teachers to government quangos? And why? And what have been the consequences for teacher-led curriculum innovation, which is the focus of this book?

Ten years on from the Schools Council's inception and the high point of professional involvement in curriculum matters which it represented, the oil crisis of 1974 and the upward spiral of youth unemployment generated certain pressures for a more centralized control of curriculum development. Schools were blamed for the failure of their pupils to find work. 'If only young people were better educated and trained, they'd get a job,' was a common refrain, ignoring completely the economic forces outside of the schools' control that had reduced the number of jobs generally available to school leavers. It simply was not possible for *all* 16-year-old leavers to get a job because there weren't enough to go round. Conveniently, politicians chose to ignore this fact. Of course, these pressures were there before the Suez Canal was blockaded during the Arab–Israeli conflict. Politicians and the media have been sniping at teachers for as long as schools have existed. The Black Papers attack on 'progressive' teaching, which ran from 1969 to 1975 (Cox and Dyson 1969), and the inevitable reaction to the student 'unrest' of 1968 and 1969 may have helped to fuel the backlash against the perceived failings of schools. And the teacher shortages of the 1950s and 1960s, which accompanied the massive expansion of secondary education, were replaced by oversupply as pupil numbers began to fall. The profession itself was vulnerable to cuts in funding.

James Callaghan's Ruskin College speech of 1976 took up employability as one of its issues and challenged the relevance to the world of work of much of what was being taught in secondary schools.

I have been concerned on my journeys to find that new recruits from schools sometimes do not have the basic skills to do the job that is required. I have been concerned to find that many of our best trained students who have completed the higher levels of education at university or polytechnic have no desire to join industry . . . there is a need to improve relations between industry and education.

(Callaghan 1976; see also Callaghan 1987)

This speech heralded the dawn of a new relationship between the government and the profession. Bernard Donoughue, Senior Policy Adviser to the

Labour Party Prime Minister at that time, in reflecting on the background to what became known as 'The Great Debate', wrote that:

> We positively relished an opportunity to breach what we regarded as the negative hold which the teacher organisations had maintained over the determination of educational objectives and practice.
>
> (Donoughue 1987)

This represented a significant shift in ministerial attitude to curriculum control. No longer was the profession to be trusted with the sort of influence it had enjoyed over the curriculum since the emergence of the Schools Council. The days when George Tomlinson, Secretary of State for Education, could declare in 1947 that 'the Minister knows nowt about the curriculum' (quoted in Kirk 1989) were over.

It was 'open season' for the curriculum.

The 'Great Debate' that followed Callaghan's speech provided for eight regional conferences at which representative groups were encouraged to discuss issues relating to the school curriculum, assessment, teacher training and the relationship between school and the world of work. Unsurprisingly, very different views were expressed, which may well have left the way clear for a more decisive lead from the centre (Kirk 1989).

The Green Paper *Education in Schools: a Consultative Document*, circulated by the DES in 1977 as a consequence of the Great Debate, heralded this move to a more centralized approach with its assertion of the need 'to establish generally accepted principles for the composition of the school curriculum for all pupils'. LEAs were asked to provide details of curriculum planning and policies. What emerged from this enquiry was that most LEAs had neither any clear policies nor any shared consensus about essential curriculum content. The government's response to this in *A Framework for the School Curriculum* (DES 1980) and *The School Curriculum* (DES 1981) made it clear that schools needed to be covering a basic core of subjects and activities, although the latter document included the reassuring statement that 'neither the government nor the local authorities should specify in detail what the schools should teach' (DES 1981).

This was also the line of HMI, whose own document *Curriculum 11–16* stated that 'it is not the intention to advocate a standard national curriculum for all secondary schools to the age of 16, not least because that would be educationally naive' (HMI 1977b). This document from the inspectorate, and successive documents such as *Aspects of Secondary Education* (HMI 1979) and *A View of the Curriculum* (HMI 1980), differed in some respects from the DES view. Although there was broad support for the idea of a common core of learning, the Inspectorate was concerned to promote an 'entitlement model' based on 'areas of experience'. The suggestion was that the curriculum should be organized in such a way that all pupils had access to eight areas of experience (aesthetic and creative, ethical, linguistic, mathematical, physical, scientific, social and political, and spiritual). The emphasis here was very much on the professional teacher being at the centre of the process of curriculum development.

For those of us working in experimental educational projects at that time, this document seemed like an official endorsement of what we'd been doing for some years – and what we'd hitherto looked upon as rather an 'alternative curriculum' model. It was a breath of fresh air. Our own LEA required us to indicate how we were addressing these eight areas of experience. In framing responses we were able to integrate our particular three Rs (Responsibility, aRticulation and Relevance) within the HMI framework, and celebrate the overlap between official 'theory' and our own 'practice'. One example may illustrate the point: we took a decision very early on that the young people who came should be involved in the day-to-day running of the school. At a very practical level this meant drawing up rotas for answering the telephone, cooking the midday meal, showing round visitors, cleaning the common room, handling the petty cash and maintaining the premises. The weekly group meeting that involved *all* staff and pupils often took some time to sort out this rota and the various problems associated with its implementation. Issues of responsibility, mutual cooperation, taking turns and 'fair shares' confronted the whole group with some challenging 'ethical and social' concepts – rooted in the reality of everyday experience (White 1980).

It came as no surprise to discover in researching documentation for *this* book that 34,000 copies of the *Curriculum 11–16* document were distributed *on request* in 1977. Twenty years later, reading Howard Gardner on 'multiple intelligences' (Gardner 1993), I am struck by the correspondence between his notion of intelligence and the HMI 'areas of experience', and wonder how different things might have been had the obsession with stated curriculum content and mistrust of professional involvement not overshadowed the debate.

In *The Sabre Toothed Curriculum* (1939) J. Abner Peddiwell describes a society experiencing the traumas of transition as a result of the Ice Age. It is a story I often offer to the student teachers with whom I work.

In the pre Ice Age culture, which was essentially a hunting and fishing community, children were inducted by their elders into the essential skills of 'catching fish with bare hands', 'clubbing woolly horses', and 'sabre-toothed tiger scaring'. This worked well for the tribe, because the scaly fish could easily be gripped by bare hands, the woolly horses were so deaf that it was possible to creep up behind them unnoticed, and the tigers were terrified by burning branches which could be lit from the camp fires and waved in their snarling faces.

Unfortunately the Ice Age came and went, bringing fundamental changes in the fauna and flora. The scaly fish were replaced by a smooth skinned variety, too slippery to grasp with bare hands; the antelopes that replaced the woolly horses were so alert and sensitive to sound that it was quite impossible to creep up unheard; and the ferocious glacial bears that became the principal predators were unaffected by blazing branches.

In spite of this, though, the core curriculum for the young people stayed the same as before, because of the reverence for the classical tradition of 'catching fish with bare hands', 'woolly horse clubbing' and 'sabre tooth tiger scaring' that had served their ancestors so well. Of course there were the occasional voices raised in protest. 'Wouldn't it be better', some argued, 'to teach our children how to catch fish with a rod and line, how to snare antelopes with springy young trees and noosed vines, and how to trap bears in deep pits?' Such solitary voices preaching curriculum revolution were silenced, their ideas ridiculed and ignored.

In Peddiwell's allegory, it was left to archaeologists to unearth the remains of that society – a few phrases carved in stone by the village elders:

You would know that the essence of true education is timelessness. It is something that endures through changing conditions, like a solid rock standing squarely and firmly in the middle of a raging torrent. You must know that there are some eternal verities, and the sabre-tooth curriculum is one of them.

(Peddiwell 1939)

Students appreciate the irony of the tale, although many dismiss it as yet another unworkable outpouring from the liberal fringe. In a culture where programmes of study, schemes of work and attainment targets predominate, it is difficult to argue for the ascendancy of another set of values. Yet, in 1977, there was a glimmer of recognition and support from one corner of officialdom for a view of how the curriculum might be structured, which differed from the notion of centralized control. It is interesting to consider how this HMI view was marginalized in the run up to the 1988 Act. And, why? Commentators such as Denis Lawton point to the conflicting ideologies within the Conservative Party and the appeasement of minority views which resulted from producing a curriculum that appealed to 'minimalists' (with its emphasis on the concept of 'core') and 'privatizers' (with its emphasis on an assessment framework that could support league tables), while ignoring the 'pluralists' (who supported the notion of entitlement). The latter, being based on HMI's Areas of Experience, was 'unfamiliar and looked suspiciously like "educational theory" – an increasingly taboo concept in right-wing circles' (Lawton 1993).

However, many schools had responded very positively to the HMI notion of an 'entitlement curriculum'. The 34,000 copies of *Curriculum 11–16* that were distributed provided the rationale for a wide variety of practical curriculum experiments throughout the UK, extending and supporting the notion of school based development, which was fast becoming the principal form of curriculum development (Eggleston 1980). The major national projects of the 1960s and 1970s, spearheaded and funded by the Schools Council, Nuffield and similar bodies, had had their day. Increasingly more localized developments were in the ascendancy, in recognition of the fact that schools and teachers themselves needed to be part of the change process.

After 1978 the emphasis on the School Council's work changed from the large scale team projects (such as GYSL and HCP) to local development projects and small scale initiatives. Five new programmes focussed on the curriculum development process . . . Two projects were specifically directed to school curriculum renewal – guidelines for review and internal development in schools (GRIDS). In Deansby and Birchwood schools the initial interest in the implementation of the GYSL project was extended to other major humanities innovations such as MACOS (Bruner). To these the teachers brought their own interpretations. Their current practice and the formulae they adopted for further innovation represented a complex and dynamic interplay between personal ideals and the expectations and constraints of the school community, wider society, and the official reality definers: LEA, DES and examination boards.

(Dalton 1988)

The trend towards mixed ability teaching within comprehensive schools was another catalyst, encouraging the development of resource centres, with teaching packs, worksheets and handouts, replacing books as the basis for classroom work. Some LEAs even established their own 'Resources for Learning Development Units' to support consortia of teachers in the production of curriculum materials for use in local schools. In this respect HMI again provided official encouragement through a whole series of papers entitled 'Matters for Discussion', beginning with *Ten Good Schools* in 1977 and following through with documents that included *Mixed Ability Work in the Comprehensive School* (1978), leading up to the *View of the Curriculum* in 1980.

Very definitely, as the 1970s moved into the 1980s, school based development (alongside school based INSET) became the dominant form of curriculum development, a fact which the Manpower Services Commission was able to exploit to the full in its invitation in November 1982 for consortia of schools to tender for funding through the Technical and Vocational Education Initiative (TVEI). The educational literature of the time abounds with examples of the prevalence of such a view. Articles in the *TES* and shelves of books were devoted to describing, explaining, analysing and drawing out disseminating principles from numerous 'case studies' of school based curriculum activities, which were often the brainchild of small groups of highly motivated staff in individual establishments. The TVEI documentation maintained the focus on school based work, highlighting examples of 'flexible learning', 'resource based learning', 'developmental group work' and other teacher-initiated approaches to the curriculum (Gleeson *et al.* 1988; Dale *et al.* 1990).

Although TVEI was the most influential and widespread programme for curriculum change for the 14–18 age group during the 1980s, it was not the only example of a national idea that LEAs and schools transformed into individualized developments. 'Active Tutorial Work' (Baldwin and Wells 1979–84; Hutchinson 1991), 'Group Tutoring' (Button 1984), 'Peace Education' (Halstead 1986), 'Somerset Thinking Skills' (Blagg 1989; 1993) and 'Mathematics in Education and Industry' (Porkess 1995) are all illustrations of ways in which individual teachers came together to tailor-make curriculum activities around particular themes that were taken up by a large number of schools across the country.

Yet within five years of the introduction of TVEI in 1983 the map of the curriculum territory was transformed by the introduction of a national curriculum alongside an assessment framework that seemed to take no notice of what had been achieved by teachers within the framework of TVEI, and that effectively suffocated endeavours of schools or LEAs to undertake any further innovative curriculum development.

How this happened so quickly is an interesting point.

The Green Paper of 1977 had given clear indications that centralized control was on the horizon, and the 1979 report on the DES enquiry into LEA provision, *Local Authority Arrangements for the School Curriculum*, proposed that the government would 'give a lead in the process of reaching a national consensus on a desirable framework for the curriculum' (DES 1979), indicating that the Labour Party was moving towards some sort of centrally influenced curriculum model. And with regard to *educational* policy, the election of the Conservative Party that same year heralded little immediate change, suggesting that some sort of consensus about curriculum structure crossed the political divide between the two major parties. The DES continued to offer ideas and guidance as to the shape of a core curriculum, and Mark Carlisle's principal contribution, as Secretary of State for Education, was to initiate the Assisted Places Scheme and preside over the beginning of what was to become a major reduction in central government expenditure on education.

Although his successor, Keith Joseph, was ideologically opposed to a national curriculum, he was in favour of more centralized control of education, as evidenced by some of his actions during his five years as Secretary of State from 1981 to 1986. He 'allowed' the introduction of TVEI in 1982, which many educational professionals regarded with great suspicion at the outset, because of its direct associations with the Department of Employment (not Education), and its clear intentions to manipulate curriculum content through rather crude reallocations of funding from a central agency, the Manpower Services Commission (MSC). He abolished the Schools Council in 1984, setting up in its place two government controlled bodies – the School Curriculum Development Committee (SCDC) and the Secondary Examinations Council (SEC).

In the same speech to the North of England conference in January 1984, in which he axed the Schools Council, Keith Joseph also made it very clear that the government intended to define the expected levels of attainment that should be achieved by pupils at different stages of schooling, would restructure the 16+ examination so as to measure absolute performance and would take steps to 'wrench the system from its prognostic connotations for the few to an achievement record for the many' (Fowler 1988). As a direct consequence, GCE and CSE were merged into a common examination, with the requirement that all of the new GCSE syllabuses had to be approved by the Secretary of State. Additional funding was provided for the development that became known as 'Records of Achievement' (DES 1984; PRAISE 1987), and for other initiatives such as the 'Lower Attaining Pupils Programme' (DES 1982; NFER 1991), known as ROAs and LAPP respectively.

By the end of his tenure of office the government had still not assumed *direct* control of the curriculum, although subsequent events were foreshadowed in *Better Schools* (DES 1985), which was the translation into action of his North of England speech.

The 5–16 curriculum needs to be constructed and delivered as a continuous and coherent whole, in which the primary phase prepares for the secondary phase and the latter builds on the former.

(DES 1985)

It was the arrival of Kenneth Baker at the Department of Science that heralded the implementation of a formalized and centrally determined national curriculum. Although the government had required LEAs to submit written policy statements for all aspects of the school curriculum in its 1986 Education Act, this was clearly not sufficient for a new Secretary of State who was sympathetic to those in his party concerned with 'standards' and arguing for more 'accountability' from schools and educational professionals (Hillgate Group 1987). The Conservative Party itself was not united behind one particular ideology, however. The differences between the 'privatizers', the 'minimalists' and the 'pluralists' (Lawton 1993) has been referred to earlier (page 11). Aware that there were such broad differences of opinion, even among his cabinet colleagues, Baker first announced his plans for a broad, national curriculum on *Weekend World* in December 1986, wrong footing opponents in his own party who favoured a narrower focus on English, mathematics and science.

One month later, in outlining the proposed 'Great Education Reform Bill' at the North of England Conference in January 1987, Kenneth Baker made it clear that the locus of control was shifting.

I believe some searching questions now need to be asked. Is it really acceptable that in the vital matter of education hardly anyone can be sure where responsibilities lie? . . . In my view the country is entitled to an education system which not only works well but is also intelligible and shows clearly where responsibility and accountability lie.

(Baker 1993)

The 1988 Education Act that resulted in the implementation of the National Curriculum and its assessment framework had few supporters among the educational establishment. The consultative paper that preceded the legislation drew nearly 12,000 responses, most of which were sharply critical of aspects of the proposals. A selection of these were published by Julian Haviland:

I can confirm that the principle [of a national curriculum] was overwhelmingly approved: I cannot recall one response, however, that endorsed without reservation the structure for the curriculum which the government was proposing.

(Haviland 1988)

Denis Lawton was one of those who drew attention to the dangers of what he saw as a 'bureaucratic approach' to the notion of a common curriculum. He encouraged the professionals to salvage the situation by insisting on

a national curriculum which concentrates on broad objectives, not detailed lists of content, and teachers being involved at school level to work out the detailed curriculum [in accordance with national guidelines].

(*TES* 1 May 1987)

Peter Cornall, Senior County Inspector for Cornwall, was more forthright:

> We have the gravely flawed product of amateurs, a hasty, shallow, simplistic sketch of a curriculum, reductionist in one direction, marginalising in another, paying only a dismissive lip service to the professional enterprise and initiative on which all progress depends.
>
> (In O'Connor 1987)

However, despite many such warnings, including those from his own party, like Keith Joseph's ('far too rigid') and Stuart Sexton's ('will put the schools' curriculum into a straitjacket'), and all the historical evidence that demonstrates how successful curriculum change needs to start from the professional concern of teachers, only tokenistic attempts were made by the Secretary of State to involve them in the process.

With the disbanding of the Schools Council in 1984, teacher involvement in the metamorphosed organizations – the SCDC and SEC – was lessened considerably. Although some of the original staff remained, and the teacher unions (particularly the NUT) retained some managerial involvement, this professional representation was rather short lived. The 1988 Act transformed the scene yet again, with the establishment of the National Curriculum Council (NCC) and the Secondary Examinations and Assessment Council (SEAC). Five years later, with the programmes of study and associated attainment targets delineated in most subjects at the respective key stages, NCC and SEAC were brought together as the Secondary Curriculum and Assessment Authority (SCAA). At the same time the long-lived Department of Education and Science (DES) was renamed the Department *for* Education (DfE), prompting Ted Wragg to comment on the back page of the *TES* about the significance of prepositional logic that clearly felt it necessary to make the point that the government wasn't actually *against* education.

The changes represented by the 1988 Act and the subsequent legislation in the 1992 and 1993 Education Acts gave the Secretary of State for Education (and now Employment) unprecedented powers to decide what should be in the curriculum, how it should be assessed, and how the results of the assessments should be reported. The fallout from these hastily conceived and politically motivated pieces of legislation is still with us. Despite four ministerial changes in the Conservative Party since Kenneth Baker (John Macgregor 1989–90; Kenneth Clarke 1990–2; John Patten 1992–4; Gillian Shephard 1994–7), there are considerable problems associated with the implementation of the National Curriculum.

Although teachers have responded very professionally to the introduction of the National Curriculum programmes of study, the confusion among the subject working groups about appropriate curriculum content and attainment targets compounded the resentment felt against the workload associated with the implementation of the assessment framework. In addition, it began to emerge during the mid-1990s that the tightly prescriptive curriculum was having a negative effect on pupil achievement in precisely those subjects at the centre of any debate over standards – the three Rs. There was some evidence that primary school reading abilities were falling, with more than half of 11-year-olds achieving below the expected target for the age group in the National Test results for 1995 (Hofkins 1996a), and 10-year-olds being two years behind pupils in Germany and Switzerland in relation to mathematical ability (Bierhoff 1996; Rafferty 1996). Secondary schools seemed to be faring no better, with 40 per cent of 14-year-old pupils showing a reading age of less than 11.

Despite the fact that these levels of attainment were materializing after 17 years of Conservative control of educational provision, the response of government ministers and the Chief Inspector for Schools was to blame poor teachers and failing schools:

> The Chief Inspector for Schools called yesterday for 15,000 incompetent teachers to be sacked to raise educational standards. Chris Woodhead said it was time to stop making excuses for poor lessons and to get rid of those who were letting their pupils down. Britain needed a 'culture change' to get tough with classroom incompetence, he said . . . Mr Woodhead has often complained of the 'stubborn one third' of lessons that Ofsted has declared below standard and in comments to be broadcast on the BBC's *Panorama* on Monday he said some 375,000 children were suffering.
>
> (Charter 1995)

> Overall standards of pupil achievement need to be raised in about half of primary and two fifths of secondary schools . . . the bad news is that there are still too many schools which are failing to give their pupils a satisfactory education.
>
> (Woodhead 1996)

two

Professional autonomy

Ever since the first Black Paper was published in 1969 (Cox and Dyson), with its criticism of 'progressive' teaching methods, it has been fashionable to blame teachers and schools for what are seen as attendant consequences of progressive methods – falling standards, truancy, drug taking, hooliganism and so on. The William Tyndale School saga of the mid-seventies, in which a group of so called 'progressive' teachers was suspended from a school that was subsequently closed, only served to fuel the controversy (Ellis *et al.* 1976, Gretton and Jackson 1976). Neville Bennett's report *Teaching Styles and Pupil Progress* (Bennett 1976), in which he 'proved' that traditional methods were more effective in terms of the three Rs, was given considerably more attention in the media than his subsequent reworking of the data several years later, which demonstrated that some of the earlier findings were significantly at variance.

Offering criticism of teachers from another perspective, James Callaghan's Ruskin College remarks about the unfocused relationship between education and the world of work (Callaghan 1976) echoed the views of Arnold Weinstock, managing director of GEC.

> Teachers ... having themselves chosen not to go into industry, often deliberately instil in their pupils a similar bias ... This is quite apart from the strong though unquantifiable impression an outsider receives that the teaching profession has more than its fair share of people who are actively politically committed to the overthrow of liberal institutions.
> (Weinstock 1976)

This attack on the inadequacies of the teaching profession in relation to the world of work, and the charge that schools were paying insufficient attention to respect for industry and wealth creation, gathered momentum during the late 1970s.

> It has in recent years become a 'truth universally acknowledged' that education should be more closely linked to the world of work and with

the country's economic performance, and there has been increasing pressure on schools to assess the relevance of their curriculum to their pupils' future working lives.

(HMI/DES 1982)

The comparison with 'our competitors' (initially EU countries, Japan and the USA, and more recently the Pacific Rim) began to feature with increasing frequency in public utterances by politicians, employers' organizations (such as the CBI) and government agencies (such as the Manpower Services Commission). In 1955 the UK's share of manufacturing output in the world was 20 per cent; by 1985 it was down to 8 per cent and still falling. Understandably there was concern as to how to arrest this decline in our industrial performance, especially as there were those, such as Martin Wiener (1985) and Corelli Barnett (1986), arguing that the root of the problem was a deep-seated, cultural disdain for engineering, manufacturing and commercial activities (apart from banking!). The challenge for any government was not simply how to change the habits of a lifetime, but how to change centuries of ingrained attitudes and structures. Elected on a groundswell of popular support in 1979 for her notion that something had to be done to put the Great back into Britain, Margaret Thatcher set about the unions and schools with gusto, ably supported by David Young, the energetic boss of the Manpower Services Commission.

The Technical and Vocational Education Initiative was the major plank in a policy that believed Britain's capabilities in terms of invention, engineering and enterprise could best be addressed through curriculum innovation of particular sorts. The City Technology College development was another example, as was the decision to make technology a core subject in the national curriculum. In addition to TVEI, this emphasis on what Charles Bailey (1984) has referred to as 'economic utility' led directly to a number of other 'work related' curriculum initiatives, including the Schools Council Industry Partnership (SCIP), Mini Enterprise, Young Enterprise and, ultimately, a national framework for the accreditation of work-related competencies – with NCVQ as the quality controller. One outcome of all this was that other vested interests (such as employers) began to exert some influence over curriculum matters, with consequences for the professional autonomy of teachers.

At the same time as elevating the significance of the 'enterprise culture' in state schools, the Conservative administration legislated for more control from the centre – as the previous chapter has illustrated. Inevitably, these ministerial-directed curriculum developments have also had a bearing on the position of teachers. Although the 'autonomous professional' is a cherished concept (enshrined in the 1944 Education Act's notion of 'partnership' between LEAs, central government and teachers), it has taken a battering in recent years – compounded by the imposition of contractual duties through the Teachers Pay and Conditions Act of 1987.

Prior to this, teachers' pay had been determined by the Burnham Committee, a forum for negotiation involving local education authority representatives, teacher union representatives, and central government, with arbitration arrangements codified in law, should the respective parties not manage to reach agreement (as happened in 1974 when the Houghton Committee recommended a rise of 35 per cent on average). However, pay negotiations were separated from conditions of service, which were governed by the 'Burgundy Book', produced by the Council of Local Education Authorities Standing Committee on Teachers (CLEA/ST).

As a direct consequence of the industrial disruption between 1984 and 1987, with teachers operating a 'work to rule' (including such things as limited cover for absent colleagues, and a restriction on extra-curricular activities), the Act of 1987 dismantled the negotiating machinery of the Burnham Committee, and established, for the first time, a direct link between what teachers were paid and the conditions they worked. Contractual duties, including 195 days and 1265 hours per year, were imposed on the profession, alongside a pay award that ended the national strikes of the preceding three years. Coupled with other developments like the introduction of GCSEs and teacher appraisal schemes, this was seen by many commentators at the time as being the last nail in the coffin for the notion of the teacher as an autonomous professional.

> The Act gives unprecedented powers to a Secretary of State to impose pay and conditions on a group of public employees with passing reference only to their employers and the unions . . . It is part of a general policy whose main purposes are to circumvent powerful national union organisations, prepare for private systems and to force down wages through the competition of worker against worker in regional labour markets.
>
> (Seifert 1987)

Jenny Ozga's analysis of the way in which the profession has become 'proletarianized' charts the process of attrition by which autonomy has been chipped away.

> In terms of the strategy of overall control of the teaching force, the insistence on the contract signals the final abandonment of indirect rule as a strategy of control. Other policy initiatives had earlier signalled such a departure, especially those that threatened teachers' licensed autonomy in the classroom: for example the reform of the exam system, the contract compliance insisted on by MSC, teacher appraisal schemes and parental choice/control. These initiatives alone, in the context of declining support for the service, made the idea of the autonomous professional teacher difficult to sustain. The pay dispute and contract made it impossible.
>
> (Ozga 1989)

As Ozga argues, though, the reality of teacher autonomy had been a short-lived concept anyway.

> One reason for the strength of the idea of teacher autonomy is the effect of the 1960s and the very public acceptance in that decade of professional control and expansionist policies in education, especially comprehensive reorganisation. In a longer view, that period, far from presenting

in an exemplary fashion the traditions of consultation, consensus and partnership in education policy making, more closely resemble a departure from a much more securely established tradition – that of control and direction from the centre, resisted and modified to varying degrees by teachers and the LEAs.

(Ozga 1989)

By 1988 the reassertion of central control and direction, and the rout of the profession, was nearing completion. Despite the overwhelming opposition to its consultative document (illustrated in Chapter 1), the government majority was such that it was able to legislate for a prescriptive curriculum which clearly delineated areas of knowledge and assessment frameworks. Not for the Conservatives was the Danish tradition which requires that 'there must be universal agreement in Parliament' for any enactment of legislation concerning schools (Bach and Christensen 1992). A simple majority was quite enough, and the Conservatives' numerical advantage in Parliament was overwhelming. Francis Pym's warning about 'large majorities leading to bad government' cost him his ministerial post in 1983, but may well have had a prophetic ring to it.

Within National Curriculum subject working groups there was often acrimonious debate about what to include in the curriculum and final recommendations were not always acceptable to the Secretary of State, even in those situations where he'd personally hand-picked the person to chair the group. In his 'Case Study: English in the National Curriculum', prepared as part of Open University course EU208, Donald Mackinnon illustrates the tensions that surrounded the development of programmes of study and attainment targets in relation to one particular subject, English. It offers remarkable insights into what was obviously a deliberate move to exclude any professional opinion that was at variance with the minister's own views. Mackinnon draws extensively on the memoirs of Kenneth Baker to illustrate his points.

To chair the Committee reviewing the teaching of English, I appointed Sir John Kingman, the Vice Chancellor of Bristol University and a distinguished scientist. It was better to appoint a scientist rather than an English specialist in order to avoid the doctrinal debates which racked university English faculties in the 1970s and 1980s. However, the Kingman report proved a disappointment, because one of its conclusions was that standard English should be regarded as merely one of several dialects . . . it appeared that even the guardians of standards had become infected with fashionable nonsense.

(Baker 1993)

As Mackinnon points out, Sir John Kingman was a mathematician not a scientist, but accuracy was not Kenneth Baker's strong point, as evidenced by his immediate response to Kingman, which was to select Professor Brian Cox to chair a replacement committee on the grounds that he'd been 'co-author of the right wing Black papers in the 1970s'. In fact Brian Cox had been co-editor of the Black Papers and was well known among English teachers for his campaign to make creative writing a central feature of the English curriculum.

Unsurprisingly, therefore, Kenneth Baker was to be disappointed again when Cox's committee produced its recommendations in 1992.

> The Group's report was not as helpful as I had hoped over the question of teaching grammar, and the attainment targets set for the ages of seven and eleven were too vague. But I did welcome their commitment to standard English and to correcting such colloquial inaccuracies as 'we was', 'he ain't done it', and 'he writes real quick'.
>
> (Baker 1993)

Mackinnon elaborates on this last point, explaining that Cox's advocacy of the teaching of standard English was *not* at the expense of devaluing a child's own dialect, or claiming that it involves bad grammar. And 'he places more trust, as far as English teaching is concerned, in the professional judgement of the great majority of teachers and linguists than in the untutored common sense of politicians and other amateurs' (Mackinnon 1996).

In writing this sentence Donald Mackinnon was simply echoing a point that Brian Cox had made in his own account of the events of that period.

> My own view is that neither Mr Baker nor Mrs Rumbold knew very much about the complex debate that has been going on at least since Rousseau about progressive education, and that they did not realise that my Group would be strongly opposed to Mrs Thatcher's views about grammar and rote learning. The politicians were amateurs, instinctively confident that common sense was sufficient to guide them in making judgements about the professional standing of the interviewees.
>
> (Cox 1992)

The debate about English didn't end there, of course, because the whole issue of what texts could be considered worthy of study in schools raged on (were Shakespeare, Dickens, Keats and Wordsworth to be considered the essential 'core', or were Mills and Boon, *EastEnders* and Jeffrey Archer to be allowed a place at high table?). But this debate was now mostly about content, as was the case for the other core and foundation subjects once the Prime Minister or the Secretary of State for Education had made various rulings like that against 'anti-racist mathematics', or that the 'history curriculum had to end twenty years before the present day'.

It is worth noting too that it was not only the politicians who were making direct interventions with regard to the framework of the National Curriculum. In describing the fight for recognition of geography as a subject, Nigel Proctor illuminates the role of civil servants in the whole process.

> The fact that the civil servants were recruited almost entirely from public schools, which had a classics/history tradition in terms of curriculum content, probably caused their failure to recognise the value of, and their prejudice against new, emerging school subjects in which they themselves had never been educated. It serves to remind us of a major anomaly that people with no direct personal experience of the state system of

education were making decisions which affected the curriculum of all the state's schools. In the present move to a National Curriculum it seems clear that, while schools may continue to take responsibility for their own detailed curricula, the broad framework will be established by the civil servants at the DES, prompted by their political masters. We shall perhaps never know to what extent the most radical policies – such as benchmark testing as part of the National Curriculum – have been imposed by the politicians for the civil servants to implement, or whether the ideas themselves originated in the DES and were proposed to the Secretary of State as potential long term strategies.

(Proctor 1988)

Nigel Proctor also draws attention to another aspect of the National Curriculum where political prejudice won the day. The assessment framework proposed by the Task Group for Assessment and Testing in its recommendations to the Minister (TGAT 1988) became transformed, from something that was originally intended to be teacher led and largely diagnostic, into a system that provided rather crude 'pencil and paper' tests that could be used as 'yardsticks' for school performance. The fear of many professionals was that these 'results' would be put in the public domain to compare school with school, a concern that led to the teacher action in 1993, which forced a limited rethink. In the words of Doug McAvoy of the National Union of Teachers:

These tests will not inform parents about their child's developments, nor will they assist teachers in diagnosing their pupils' educational needs . . . they can never serve educational purposes, designed as they are to be turned into league tables of school performance.

(*Independent* 3 September 1993)

With the publication of the Dearing Review early in 1994, it seemed that the threat to put the results of these tests in the public domain had abated. However, the issue was revived with Gillian Shephard's announcement in February 1996 that raw data from the summer's test results for 11-year-olds would be published each January (Hofkins and Hackett 1996). Although this proposition again provoked bitter hostility from the profession, and the possibility of concerted attempts by Headteachers to obstruct the process (Pyke 1996a), it came as no surprise to secondary school teachers. They have been accustomed to the annual media production of 'league tables', culled from the DfEE's statistics, which give the percentage of pupils in year 11 of each school who manage to achieve five A–C grade GCSEs. The pernicious effects of these tables can hardly be overstated. Justifying its actions in producing the statistics, with the claim that these give parents accurate information about a school's performance (ignoring completely all the weight of evidence and advice about the significance of a 'value added' assessment), the government has succeeded in overlaying the ideology of the market place on formal education, with itself as the arbiter of what counts for quality.

The result has been predictable. Some 25,000 individual cost centres now compete with each other for customers. Education has become a commodity to be bought and sold, schools and colleges have become the providers of a service to consumers, teachers have become the deliverers of a curriculum to the specification of the government, delivery is evaluated against performance indicators created by the market regulators (who are not the professionals) and institutions are audited to check on the mechanisms of quality control.

The partnership in the late 1990s is between government prescribing very detailed regulations about what should be learnt, parents who have been given, in theory at least, the power to choose from a diversity of schools and employers through sponsorship and membership of governing bodies and Education Business Partnerships. As the Secretary of State said in the White Paper *Choice and Diversity*: 'Parents know best the needs of their children – certainly better than educational theorists or administrators, better even than our mostly excellent teachers' (DfE 1992).

Teachers themselves have resented attempts to downplay their role or to undermine their status, and have not been entirely passive in their response. As an illustration of the tension that has existed between policy makers and classroom teachers in recent years, a brief glance at the letters pages of the *Times Educational Supplement* in the aftermath of the presentation of the Chief Inspector's annual report for 1995 reveals the depth of feeling among the profession.

> On the strength of his oversimplistic views and arrogant statements, hundreds of thousands of teachers are left feeling tainted and depressed. How does his admiration for whole class teaching square with the needs of a mixed ability class in primary schools, and the requirement to deliver a 10 subject national curriculum, properly differentiated? Were Mr Woodhead the education correspondent of the *Daily Mail* his behaviour would seem appropriate.
>
> (Taverner 1996)

> How long can this constant battle of half truths continue? How can it be that no-one in these lofty positions of power can actually see what is happening on the ground in every school in this country? . . . Why are so many junior and primary teachers retiring early from stress related illness? Why is there a rush of secondary teachers to take advantage of early retirement once the 'magic' age of 50 is reached? . . . I have taught English in a range of secondary schools for 28 years. I have never known such a sense of outrage at what is happening in schools today . . . Every week teachers bow under yet another attack on their collective self esteem. 'Teach morality', 'Teach sport', 'Return to basics', 'More of the didactic, less of the trendy' . . . the list goes on . . . Finally I am told that large class sizes make no real difference. Ask anybody who has ever stood in front of any class – ask the caretaker.
>
> (Heys 1996)

As some commentators pointed out at the time, there is a very real danger that the wide media coverage given to criticisms of poor teachers and failing schools begins to affect both the public perception of teachers and the self-perception of teachers themselves, with direct consequences for the notion of the autonomous professional. As anyone who has read the literature on self-esteem is aware, telling people they're failures is not the most effective way of encouraging greater effort.

> Mr Woodhead's breathtakingly simplistic utterances are demotivating, demoralising and destructive to the vast number of teachers who work unstintingly on behalf of their pupils. He appears to believe that carping criticism is a model for success and perhaps has forgotten or never learned, that praise, recognition and reward form a more productive climate for development. What would we say of parents who rubbished, derided and publicly decried their child's efforts to write, speak or tackle sums?
>
> (West 1996)

> I'm slow to anger but the utterances of the Chief Inspector, and his sneering contempt for anyone who disagrees with him, has roused me to a cold fury not experienced in my 26 years in the profession . . . He has obviously not yet grasped that it tends to be the better teachers (the majority) who worry most about inspections. They are naturally self-critical and are constantly re-evaluating their own teaching perform-ance. His comments do nothing for their morale. Has it not occurred to him that many, perhaps most, of those teachers now leaving the profes-sion are among the best?
>
> (Laycock 1996)

In contrast to the reportage of Chris Woodhead's speeches, the Chief Inspec-tor for Wales offered a more positive view of the profession's achievements, demonstrating that 'breathtakingly simplistic utterances' may not yet have managed to cross Offa's Dyke.

> I am pleased to be able to report improvements in the quality of edu-cation provided by schools and in the standards achieved by pupils . . . I don't think incompetent teachers are a major problem. That's a very small proportion . . . The challenges faced by teachers need to be recog-nised and their work valued.
>
> (Roy James, Chief Inspector for Wales, quoted in Pyke 1996b)

And north of the border the situation is even more optimistic, with the Scottish Inspectorate seeing its job as about increasing the professionalism of teachers.

> Where Woodhead characterises teachers as impervious to change, the Scottish Office characterises them as capable of significant development and change . . . Where Woodhead sees teacher educators as dangerously trendy, the Scottish Office sees them as important contributors.
>
> (Harrison 1996).

There are 440,000 teachers and lecturers employed in the UK. As the com-ments in Chapter 7 illustrate, there are very deep-seated feelings among this group of people that their status and their professional autonomy have been reduced and undermined. On the measures of performance rated by the policy makers, teachers have been consistently 'delivering the goods' year on year. In the 1950s A level pass rates were about 3 per cent of the age cohort; in the 1990s they passed the 30 per cent mark. Independent evaluations have demonstrated that GCSE pass rates have been rising steadily since the introduction of the examination in 1986, and that this is *not* because the marking has become more lenient or the examinations easier. To focus attention on '15,000' failing teachers is to diminish the tremendous achievements of the remaining 425,000. Of course, if you are a parent with a child in a primary (or secondary) school class where the teaching is less effective than your experience of previous years' teachers, you will feel concerned and want action to be taken. Inevitably, too, the levels of achievement in some of the 25,000 schools in England and Wales could be improved. But such concerns and such action need to be set in the context of the structural, organizational and curricular constraints within which teachers are working.

As later chapters reveal, there is another way of approaching the issue – which is to celebrate the very real achievements of teachers and lecturers working under some challenging circumstances, and draw on this groundswell of inspiration and professional commitment for solutions to the problems confronting schools today.

Before we consider these achievements, though, it may be helpful to look at some of the underlying factors that account for the kind of heated debates witnessed in the pages of the *Times Educational Supplement*, or on the television screen whenever 'education' is the focus of attention. What is behind the collective anger of the profession in its response to the notion of 'failing schools' and 'failing teachers'? What drives Secretaries of State to lambast teachers and 'trendy methods'? What fuels the passion which all the other interest groups – including parents, employers, pupils and universities' admissions tutors – bring to debates about education?

three

Curriculum ideologies and underpinning values

The quite radical changes in education over the past thirty years, which have been outlined in the previous chapters, reflect different influences and pressures – from governments, from teachers, from employers, from parents, as well as from the students themselves. And they also reflect quite different responses to the context in which education and training are taking place.

At the heart of this are various conflicting beliefs about the purposes that education should serve and the values that it should embody.

The furore over testing arrangements and league tables, which came to a head in the summer of 1993, when the combined voices of parents and teachers persuaded the government to reconsider the situation, was a good illustration of values in conflict. Should assessment at any of the key stages be used primarily to indicate which schools are performing well, or should its principal purpose be to provide feedback on pupil progress?

Beliefs over 'freedom of choice' can collide with principles about 'equality of opportunity', as evidenced by the consternation within the Labour Party during 1995 and 1996 as Tony Blair and Cherie Booth, Harriet Harman and Jack Dromey, and Karen and Michael Barber decided to 'opt out' from their local comprehensive schools.

> The goal for policy for state education has to be to make schools good enough to attract parents who simply want the best education for their children. I am aware that the decision we are making makes that less likely. Every parent that opts out makes the improvement of state comprehensive schools more difficult.
>
> (Michael Barber, quoted in Hackett 1996)

Other examples of conflicting values are not hard to find. On the one hand, there is a desire to raise standards in core curriculum subjects – particularly those related to the three Rs. On the other hand, there are concerns about the lack of preparation of young people with regard to the skills, competencies and qualities that are needed in the wider world of work or further education.

Notions of cooperation and competition can sit uneasily side by side in a school classroom, or between neighbouring schools, when funding, staffing and maybe even the survival of the school itself depend on demonstrating expertise in a defined range of performance indicators.

With regard to the curriculum, people like Raymond Williams, Denis Lawton and Stephen Ball have written eloquently about underpinning ideologies. In *The Long Revolution* (1961), for example, Raymond Williams identified 'public educators', 'old humanists' and 'industrial trainers' as the three ideological positions still in operation. In Chapter 1 I referred to Denis Lawton's analysis of the consequence of the ideological contradiction within the Conservative Party (Lawton 1993), and such contradictions are clearly as evident within the Labour Party as it struggles to redefine its position with regard to comprehensive education, selection, parental choice and standards of achievement in the process of establishing its education policy for its first term of office after 18 years on the sidelines.

This conflict in values is reflected in various 'position papers' and policy documents. On the one hand, for secondary schools, we have had the vision of Major's administration, as presented in the White Paper *Choice and Diversity* (DfE 1992). This focused on five 'great themes' (quality, diversity, increased parental choice, greater autonomy for schools and greater accountability by schools), transforming control of education from LEAs to government quangos and encouraging the operation of 'market forces' among and between schools. On the other hand, we have had the 'alternative White Paper' *Education: a Different Vision* (IPPR 1993), produced by 14 professors of education, and stressing values such as altruism, cooperation and fairness. From a third perspective, taking a broad view of the economic needs of the UK, came *Learning to Succeed*, the 1993 report of the National Commission on Education, with its seven goals (universal nursery education; courses and qualifications which bring out the best in every pupil; every pupil to have the right to good teaching; lifetime entitlement to learning; integration of education and training; increased public and private investment in education; rise in levels of achievement). And, in 1995, the Labour Party produced *Excellence for Everyone*, affirming its commitment to the promotion of 'equality of opportunity'.

For the tertiary sector, we have had the White Paper *Education and Training for the 21st Century* (DES 1991), which established the now familiar 'three track' system; the various documents from the London Institute of Education, such as *Unifying the Post-compulsory Curriculum* (Young *et al.* 1995), arguing the case for a 'unified curriculum' post-16; from the IPPR presenting the vision of a *British Baccalaureate* (Finegold *et al.* 1990) to replace the divided and divisive programmes on offer beyond the compulsory schooling phase, from the Further Education Unit with *A Framework for Credit* (FEU 1995) and from the Secondary Heads Association with *16–19 Pathways to Achievement* (1994); alongside trenchant criticism from some quarters of the rigour, depth and breadth of the knowledge required for NVQs and GNVQs (*All Our Futures*, Channel 4 documentary December 1993).

With an eye on progression across the 16 plus divide, we have had *14–19 Strategy for the Future: the Road to Equality* (NUT 1995a), *14–19 Education and Training* (Crombie White *et al.* 1995), *Learning for the Future* (Richardson *et al.*

1995), *Education and Training 14–19: Chaos or Coherence?* (Halsall and Cockett 1996) and the Dearing Review of 16–19 provision (DfEE 1996). All of these challenged the notion of the academic–vocational divide, and the existing hierarchy of status attached to certain courses at the expense of others (although the Dearing review was rather more circumspect on this issue).

It is sometimes difficult, when confronted with educational arguments from the left and right, to ascertain precisely what are the guiding principles driving reform and change. This needs to be done, however, so that stated aims and objectives can be carefully evaluated against subsequent outcomes.

Answers to the question posed at the beginning of Chapter 1 – 'Who should decide what should be taught in schools?' – will depend entirely on the value position of the respondent; and any debate about curriculum priorities needs to be prefaced by discussion about these underpinning values. 'What sort of society do we actually want?' may be one way to reveal the differences.

In asking such questions about the nature of society we are, of course, entering the realms of philosophy. Although it has been much derided in recent years (from some quarters) as an appropriate component of teacher 'training' courses, the study of philosophy is crucial to any exploration of goals and outcomes. Debate about the purposes of education needs to be lifted beyond facile platitudes such as John Major's party conference speech in 1993.

> Like parents up and down the country I want schools to get the basics right first. To teach children how to read, how to write and [pause for emphasis] how to add up. To teach them respect and teach them discipline. And the difference between right and wrong.
>
> (Major 1993)

Such simplistic remarks actually compound the problem, because they suggest that debate about ends and means can best be conducted using the language of *The Sun*, which does little to extend the level or quality of public discourse about the issue. Playing on parental fears for political advantage does nothing to address root causes of concerns about 'standards', or 'discipline', or any of the other overarching issues that matter to parents *and* teachers in our educational system. For politicians to express a deep concern about 'back to basics', while ignoring mounting evidence of the consequences of years of neglect of school buildings, or the negative impact of aspects of the imposed national curriculum on these very basics (particularly at primary school level), or the difficulties for teachers confronting huge class sizes and reduced budgets – all of which are the *direct result of government policy* – is disingenuous.

> As a result of a disgraceful failure to invest over a 20 year period, the quality of our school buildings is often shocking, even though many good schools work tremendously hard with what they've got. The excuse that times have been hard is certainly not acceptable. Those same 20 years have seen the sale of many publicly owned companies. As Harold Macmillan put it, the family silver has been sold off. The most scandalous in a long line of such sales is the Railtrack flotation under

which the entire rail network is being sold off for a mere £1.8 billion, just over one month's spending on schools. Any sensible strategic policy on public assets should surely have involved investing some of the proceeds of the sale of this century in the public assets we are keeping and will need in the 21st century. Yet capital investment in schools has been reduced. There is now a backlog of repairs which requires up to £3.2 billion to address.

(Barber 1996)

In the rush to outdo the other, both major political parties are stressing the importance of standards, discipline, competition and choice, as if any of these concepts are value free. 'The best for every child and the best from every child,' asserted the Prime Minister to the party faithful at the Blackpool conference in 1993. Who can argue with this? Except to ask what is meant by 'best'. And who decides anyway? The driving force seems to be an overriding concern with Britain's economic performance as underlined in the White Paper on *Competitiveness* (Department of Employment 1994).

The value system behind such approaches and policies needs to be opened up for public debate. In the same way that publicly owned assets have been transferred into private hands, government funds for state education have been transferred into the private sector and the 'opted out' sector on a massive scale. The assisted places scheme and the differential per capita funding for grant maintained schools are just two examples. Government spending on the former was £93 million for 33,000 young people in 1995–6 compared to a *total* spending on its school building programme of £342 million for 8,000,000 young people. For the three-year period 1994–7 the government ensured that grant maintained schools received almost double the capital funding for other schools (around £110 per capita, compared to £65 per local authority pupil).

While recognizing that there is no absolute right or wrong about such policies, we need to be able to examine the goals to which such policies are being directed – the kind of society that is intended as an outcome. We heard a lot about the 'classless society', for instance, in the early 1990s, and we were told that the assisted places scheme was an opportunity for 'able' working class children to experience the high quality education that only the well off could afford. However, evidence provided by studies of the assisted places scheme, particularly the research conducted by Tony Edwards, John Fitz and Geoff Whitty (1989) demonstrates that this has manifestly not been happening. The beneficiaries of the scheme appear to be largely the divorced or separated middle classes. Whether this is 'right' or 'wrong' is not the issue; what matters is that what is happening is not in accordance with the line that the government has fed the public.

What sort of society will be the outcome of educational policies of the past 20 years? Will it be more or less cohesive? And does that matter? Do we share the view espoused by Margaret Thatcher in 1984 that 'there is no such thing as society'? Do we agree with John Major's remark in 1992, in response to media reportage of delinquent behaviour among young people, that 'society must condemn a little more and understand a little less'?

Such statements reveal so much about the value system that underpinned the Conservative administration. It was one that excluded groups of people. In educational terms it is a value system that supports selection and restricted access; that marginalizes school refusers and disruptive pupils; that celebrates individual as opposed to community advancement; that results in an expansion of private schooling at the expense of the public sector; that acknowledges and even celebrates the concept of a 'sink school', because the 'market place' will operate to resolve the problem. It is a value system that has consequences for the kind of society our children will inherit. And it is a value system that is not necessarily shared by educational policy makers in other countries around the world, as illustrated in the next chapter.

In the spring of 1982, I took several months' unpaid leave for an African journey that led me from Lusaka in Zambia to Bulawayo in the newly independent Zimbabwe, and on to Francestown and Gabarone in Botswana. At one point I had the opportunity to join a Catholic priest from a local mission on a journey into 'the bush'. In a small village, 30 miles from the main road between Sesheke and Livingstone, I was offered food by the wife of the headman. Her daughter proudly held up the struggling chicken that had been selected. While waiting for it to be skinned and cooked, I was shown round the village by one of her sons. He indicated the vast expanse of open ground beyond the thatched rondavels that had once been a lake.

'Even five years ago, we could catch enough fish to live off. Now the water has dried up. And, unless it rains soon, we shall have no maize to harvest. All that we have left is what you see in the stores. That will soon be gone.' He pointed to the raised hut, where the level of dried cobs and husks was close to the floor.

'What will you do then?' I asked, with the sort of naivete that comes from a culture gap of thousands of miles and years of experiences.

'Die,' he replied, 'What else can we do?'

At the time I was reading Ali Mazrui's *The African Condition*, the subject of the 1979 Reith Lectures.

The moral duty of every family in the northern hemisphere is not to leave its children materially even better off than they have been, but to plan for a slight impoverishment of the next generation of westerners. The western world already consumes far too much of what there is on the planet, without planning for much more.

(Mazrui 1980)

Now and again I try to remind myself of the road I once travelled, which it is easy to gloss over in a culture where the 'consumer' rules, and where 'growth' is reified.

It is 40 years since Erich Fromm pointed out that wealth creation as an end in itself was destructive of justice, morality and a proper humanity (Fromm 1956). Yet in its pursuit of wealth creation the current government has reified 'competitiveness' and 'growth' into unassailable gods – essential worshipping for true believers in a modern economy, even though 'cooperation' and 'sustainable development' could be considered more appropriate to the global world of 1997.

On current information we know that the world's oil reserves will run out in about 50 years, within the lifetime of most children currently at school. The supply of phosphates, that essential ingredient of fertilizers, will be exhausted at about the same time. We know that every year an area the size of the Republic of Ireland becomes useless as farmland; we know that water supplies are diminishing, as the world population increases by 90 million each year (Radford 1996). We know all these things and we know that the world our grandchildren are destined to inherit will have to be much more careful than we are about its use of resources. Arguably such concerns should permeate the curriculum of all schools in preparation for this future reality.

Charles Bailey's critique of the notion of 'economic utility' has already been referred to in Chapter 2, but it is relevant to mention it again in this context. Bailey's concern (expressed in 1984) was about the consequences for education if the free market became the principal determinant of resource allocation.

It seems particularly one-sided to judge an educational system by the simple criterion of contribution to wealth creation for two main reasons. First because educators must be duty bound to introduce pupils to con-troversial matters *as* controversial matters; and secondly because schools of liberal education must introduce pupils to those activities and prac-tices which can be considered as worthwhile in themselves and therefore fit to be considered as ends rather than means.

(Bailey 1984)

How willing are the policy makers and curriculum designers to recognize the need for public debate over the 'ends' of education? And how prepared are they to admit that other value systems might be worth considering?

Interviewed on *Women's Hour* on BBC Radio 4 shortly after his appoint-ment as Chancellor of the Exchequer in 1992, Kenneth Clarke reminisced about some of the factors that had led him into politics in the 1960s, when the Labour Party was in power. 'I was afraid that we might have gone the same way of the socialist Scandinavians – thank God we didn't.' Were we to visit Denmark today we would find:

- an economy that is one of the strongest in Europe, where the *manufacturing* base of the country is booming;
- a primary *health care* system that provides universal, free treatment within a nationally coordinated framework where private practice is not encouraged;
- an *education* system that enables more than 90 per cent of 16-year-olds to continue with further education and training;
- a *welfare* system that ensures maternity benefits for 26 weeks, universal pre-school provision, earnings related unemployment benefits that equal 90 per cent of a person's terminal wage for seven years, and guaranteed support for skill retraining;
- a *transport* system that provides a regular, reliable, clean, *state run* network of buses, trains and boats to service the 458 islands that constitute Denmark;
- *streets* and *roads* in the cities that are generally devoid of litter or dog crap or homeless beggars.

On the issues by which our own Conservative Party would most like to have been judged for their competence (the economy and law and order), Denmark does rather well. In 1995 unemployment was 9 per cent (compared to an overall 13 per cent in the UK), the balance of payments was £4 billion in the black (compared to the UK's £18 billion in the red), incidence of serious crime was one-quarter that of the UK per head of population (*Danmarks Statistik* 1995). And in the International Institute for Management Development's assessment of comparative 'competitiveness' of industrialized countries in 1996, the UK had fallen to nineteenth, while Denmark had risen to fifth (Ryle and White 1996).

Of what was Kenneth Clarke so fearful?

The guaranteed minimum wage of 81 kroner (£9.00) an hour perhaps? The requirement that *every* employer must provide toilet facilities for employees and a separate space where food can be prepared at break times? The expectation that employers and employees will invest in training and retraining? The average working week of 37 hours for those employed in manufacturing industry (compared to the 45 worked in the UK) (Eurostat 1991)? Or a system of taxation that means a person will pay more than 50 per cent of earnings?

The *social democracy* that has predominated in Denmark since the war has been preserved by politicians from parties of both the left and the right, with the population consistently voting for manifestos committed to maintaining a high level of taxation.

Why is this? How is it that a whole population can sustain an attitude to taxation that ensures the base level is more than *twice* that of the UK? Are the Danes any less self-interested than us Brits? And is there any connection between the visible outcomes of 50 years of social democracy as depicted above in Denmark and its system of education?

For ten years student teachers from the Faculty of Education at the University of the West of England have taken part in an exchange programme with a Danish teacher training college in Denmark. Following an intensive week of study visits to a range of schools and colleges, the students undertake a practical placement for several months in selected establishments. What has consistently emerged from this experience is the *profound* impact this exchange has had on their perceptions and beliefs (White and Drower 1993).

In examining the education system the British student teachers are surprised to discover that Denmark is a country where:

- teachers are not encouraged to teach children to read until the age of 7, yet adult illiteracy levels are among the lowest in Europe;
- some schools don't possess even one computer, yet Danish business technology is at the cutting edge of development in the world;
- all pupils are taught in mixed ability groups from the age of 6 to 16 in almost all subjects;
- a pupil may stay with the same class and class teacher throughout almost the whole of his or her period of compulsory schooling;
- pupils call teachers by first names and uniform is unheard of;

- every 16-year-old has the right to remain in further education and continue with academic or vocational studies equivalent to our A levels or GNVQs, whether or not he or she takes the national examination for school leavers;
- the first national 'tests' that young people experience are the 'optional' examinations at 16, yet levels of ability in mathematics and other subjects compare favourably with those demonstrated by young people in the UK;
- anyone can start a school and be assured of around 85 per cent of the running costs from the government, whatever the political shade of the school.

Even the mere *suggestion* that some of these could be considered for our own schooling system would set alarm bells ringing throughout the educational establishment. Abandoning uniform, pupils using teachers' first names and not teaching reading until 7 would be seen as presaging a return to the Dark Ages. Indiscipline, disrespect and illiteracy would be headlined as inevitable consequences.

Yet this doesn't happen in Denmark.

What is even more remarkable is that the *opposite* appears to be happening – and the outcome is a cohesive, well educated and socially responsible population (although Peter Hoeg's novels offer some perspectives on the 'shadow side' of Denmark).[1] Is there something we could learn from the Danish value base? At the very least could we not collectively consider the importance of informed public debate about values and beliefs – about the 'ends' and 'means' of education?

In his book *Closing the Gap: Liberal Education and Vocational Preparation* (1995a), Richard Pring provides a careful and critical analysis of the whole issue of 'underpinning values'.

> The purposes of education, the content of educational programmes, the standards by which educational progress is judged, the idea of the educated person itself are all permeated by feelings and judgements of value. Ultimately it all depends on one's view of the life worth living. But there is no certain answer to these central questions of value. Education therefore cannot be a programme of learning that takes those values for granted.
>
> (Pring 1995a)

The 'philosophical' insights offered in his book help to illuminate the way forward. There is no suggestion of an absolute right or wrong course of action, rather a plea for clarity about desired outcomes, and an informed and public debate about what these are. In Isaiah Berlin's famous phrase, we need to 'simply worry it out' (Berlin in Magee 1978).

Richard Pring explores the differences between the 'liberal educators' and the 'vocational trainers', identifying four separate strands to arguments about the purpose of education: intellectual excellence, social utility, pursuit of pleasure and interests. In his view this separation between the academic and the vocational, between theory and practice, between education and training is a false dichotomy. And there is plenty of evidence that the profession broadly supports this view.

Many teachers are suspicious of intellectual excellence as the sole or main aim of education, just as they are of economic usefulness. Those suspicions emerge from the frequently voiced view that all children are important even though they may not aspire to excellence in academic matters or economic usefulness. Children are *persons*, and to be a person is more than to have an intellect; it is to have emotions and feelings, to enter into relationships, to have desires and aspirations, to have responsibilities and obligations. Moreover to be recognised as a person requires being treated not simply as someone with great academic potential nor as a means to an end such as the economic success of society. Too many children have been dismissed as unimportant because they are unable to succeed academically – to enter into that intellectual conversation that has been defined by people in positions of academic control.

(Pring 1995a)

In Richard Pring's terms, being a 'whole person' requires knowledge and understanding, intellectual virtues, imagination, intellectual skills, self-reflection, moral virtues and habits, social and personal involvement, and integrity and authenticity. The book as a whole is a challenge to traditional notions of what it means to be educated.

The *Who's Who* measure of 'educated', which simply refers to the (usually) high status institutions that the referenced person has attended, obscures the need for a more critical exploration of the concept itself. It is perfectly possible to pass through the portals of the most prestigious schools and universities in the country and come out with an intellect impoverished in a whole range of important human attributes. Many of the problems that concern people at a day-to-day level are to do with interpersonal relationships and their relationships towards structures and 'things' – like money. Soap operas are about love and hate, marriage and divorce, jealousy and betrayal, power and evil, the quick and the dead. Many of our fundamental problems as human beings revolve around communication – or lack of it – with our fellow men and women, and the eminent academic in the 'ivory tower', the captain of industry or the Secretary of State is as much subject to these problems as the factory worker or the shop assistant – and no better equipped to deal with them simply by virtue of academic qualifications or vocational certificates.

As long as we continue to accept the 'reification' of certain forms of knowledge (Young and Whitty 1977), we allow access to money, work and status to be determined by a narrow range of indicators that suit particular interest groups. Of the £16 billion spent on education each year, it is interesting to reflect on how unequally it is distributed among the different 'consumer' groups. A young person who continues through 13 years of schooling and then into university will have twice as much state funding spent on him or her as someone who leaves school at 16. And what determines the opportunity to receive such additional monies is performance at GCSEs. Failure to achieve the requisite number of examination grades that unlock the door to further and higher education is put down to individual pathology. It is the students' own fault if they screw up their GCSEs. 'If only I'd worked harder or been cleverer, things might have been very different,' is an oft repeated cry. The standard by which success or failure is adjudged by others is never questioned, so that the populist call to 'raise standards' favoured by all political parties seems to brook no challenge. But, as Richard Pring (1995a) points out, this simplistic deception impoverishes any debate about standards in our schools.

> Teachers feel aggrieved at seeing standards defined entirely in terms of academic excellence when they know that there is much more to being a person than that. Academic excellence so defined does little justice to the intellectual qualities necessary for exercising the range of capacities attributable to being a person.

The same point was made by Bob Moon in a letter to *The Guardian* in March 1996, taking issue with David Blunkett's speech to the Social Market Foundation in which he had outlined Labour Party policy:

> Finally, the speech makes much of school standards and improvements. But improvement towards what? It has to be something more than raising the percentage obtaining A–C grade GCSEs. How can schools set up a vision of the future that reflects the personal opportunities and civic responsibilities of the 21st century? And how does the future of education link with other social and economic policies? There is much to be done. Schools and teachers need to be on board for that debate.

During the first half of 1996 Richard Pring organized a series of open lectures at Oxford University around the theme of 'affirming the comprehensive ideal'. With contributions from Denis Lawton, Ted Wragg, Caroline Benn and other educational writers, thinkers and practitioners, the whole series challenged the analysis of certain Conservative *and* Labour politicians that the comprehensive experiment had failed: 'successive generations of children and enforced drab uniformity in the name of fairness' (Blunkett quoted in Burstall 1996).
Central to their challenge was the issue of values.

> The comprehensive system is an enactment of values like equity and inclusiveness. The Conservatives have introduced a new value system which emphasises the market, competition, excellence, social mobility and performance. It's a form of barbarianism.
>
> (Ball quoted in Hodges 1996)

In urging those charged with formulating educational policy to examine critically aims and values, the lecture series was making the point that there is and can never be any certainty about what these values and beliefs ought to be. The danger lies in any one party or interest group laying claim to the 'truth' about what needs to be taught and learnt in schools. Such arrogance negates the importance of the discussion and disagreement that is part of a healthy debate in a pluralist society. The current situation, where a small group of politicians, advised by a select band of civil servants and 'spin doctors' (awful phrase!), has absolute power to determine what is taught to whom and for how long, is a recipe for disaster. As schools are increasingly being judged by the language of the market place, where the performance indicators are defined around a very narrow range of standards, it is inevitable that some schools and some teachers will be deemed to be 'failing'. In narrowing the focus on what counts in the assessment of successful schools, the ideology that drives the process is one that consigns large numbers of young people to the rubbish tip.

Twenty years previously, in *The Sociology of the School Curriculum*, John Eggleston distinguished between the 'received perspective' and the 'reflexive perspective'.

> The received perspective is not just a dominant one. It is one in which curriculum knowledge, like other components of the knowledge system in the social order, is accepted as a received body of understanding that is 'given', even ascribed ... The reflexive perspective is one in which curriculum knowledge, like the components of the knowledge system, is seen to be negotiable; in which content can be legitimately criticized and argued or new curricula devised. Together the two perspectives represent polar views on the nature of social control and the distribution of power in society; curriculum being but one component of the inter-related arrangements for order in the social system.
>
> (Eggleston 1977)

In marginalizing the 'reflexive perspective', and in excluding teachers from the debate about what should be taught in schools and why, there is a real danger of driving the National Curriculum bandwagon into a moral blind alley. Teachers often express unease about the 'market place' ideology that forces schools into becoming competing cost centres, where excellence is adjudged on a range of performance indicators that are increasingly being reduced to the lowest common denominator of numbers of pupils gaining five A–C grades at GCSE, irrespective of the nature of the intake to the school. Little notice is taken of the school's record of success on a whole set of other indicators, like creative or sporting achievements, or moral atmosphere. Perhaps this blinkered view of success jars with a body of people who have a deep seated commitment to the importance of the *affective* as well as the *cognitive* domain. Indeed, new recruits to the profession, including escapees from industry and commerce, are often attracted to teaching precisely because it is about working *with* people.

Increasingly, these new recruits and many of those attending further professional development courses are introduced to the concept of the 'reflective practitioner' (Schon 1983; Pollard and Tann 1993), where the individual teacher is encouraged to see himself or herself at the centre of a dynamic process in the classroom. Kolb's cycle of experience, reflection and reformulation (Kolb 1984) is at the heart of this process at all levels of the education system, and there are plenty of signs that this impacts enormously on practice – a practice which is influenced by personal beliefs and constructs.

> Teachers have a strong sense of values. They teach because they believe in something, and they want to see it conveyed. They have a conception of the 'good life' and the 'good citizen'. They know what kind of society

they would like, what kind of personal and social values they wish to encourage, what knowledge they wish to convey, and how. All these things are interconnected. Teaching is, at heart, a moral craft.

(Woods 1995)

Of course there's a danger, in representing and analysing teacher's views, of suggesting a commonality of opposition to recent reforms. That manifestly is not the case, and it's important to acknowledge that teachers don't necessarily share the same values, even if they mostly share the notion of 'commitment', as Máirtín Mac an Ghaill (1992a) illustrated with his study of teachers' reactions to the 1988 Act.

In another article published in 1992, Máirtín Mac an Ghaill drew attention to another dimension of the issue of curriculum innovation, which has been largely ignored in the debate about relevance and appropriateness: the perspective of the students themselves. What did *they* think about the impact and the consequences of the National Curriculum? And how involved did they feel in the decision making processes that reflected the value base of the school (Mac an Ghaill 1992b).

One of the 'underpinning values' of the Bayswater Centre referred to in the Preface was a belief in the importance of involving the pupils in the running of the school – a belief that they had a need (and a right) to take an active part in the decision-making processes that permeated the daily work of the school. On Friday morning all staff and students came together to review the week. It was an opportunity to raise concerns and problems, and talk them through to some conclusion; it was also the time to allocate individual 'areas of responsibility' for the week ahead. Of course, there were limitations on the power that the pupils could wield and we held many of the trump cards by virtue of our age and authority. Nevertheless, they could and did make some important decisions that affected the day-to-day activities and atmosphere within the school. Inevitably there were conflicts and these weekly meetings were rarely easy. But in reflecting on their time at the Bayswater Centre, ex-pupils often asserted how important it was to them to be able to take responsibility and make real decisions.

You couldn't dodge it. You had to listen to other people's point of view. You had to be involved. The responsibility thing was important. It helped us grow up . . . prepare us for the real world.

(Ian, now a care worker in an elderly persons' home)

The story of the Bayswater Centre, as told in *Absent with Cause* (White 1980), further illustrates the point about value systems, since journal reviews of this book revealed widely differing beliefs about the purposes of education. Under the heading 'Banal lesson', Max Morris wrote:

Mr White's lessons of truancy, unoriginal to the point of banality, have little bearing on what is necessary for the normal pupil, and his conclusions are so thin and unsubstantial as to be almost unnoticeable. He is long on propaganda and description and short on analysis and practical suggestions.

(Morris 1981)

David Hargreaves's review, entitled 'Three new Rs', was rather different in tone and substance.

> Much has been written on the secondary school curriculum since the Great Education Debate, but I have read nothing more imaginative and practical than Roger White's book. This is in part because he so rightly refuses to divorce curricular issues from their social context . . . we are still in the early stages of the evolution of the comprehensive school and Roger White has, from a hidden corner of the system, helped us to specify the directions in which we ought to grow.
>
> (Hargreaves 1980)

Of course, you'd expect the value system of the President of the National Union of Teachers to be different from that of the then Reader in Education at Oxford University Department of Educational Studies. Disagreement about a book that challenged some of the presuppositions of the secondary school curriculum was inevitable.

In the wider world of education such disagreements are equally inevitable, with 'right' and 'wrong' having no absolute standards. All we can do is be as honest as possible in 'tackling the controversial issues', accepting that discussion and debate about our personal beliefs are central to the process of reaching some kind of consensus, despite the differences.

> We need to ask fundamental moral questions about what it is to live fully human lives and what the connection is between personal development and the wider social framework in which that development might take place . . . To ensure that these moral questions are not suppressed by those, including the government, who wish to subvert education to their own political or vocational ends, the ideals of this more generous concept of liberal education need to be preserved within a 'community of educated persons'. Such a community includes academics, artists, writers, scientists certainly who maintain and advance those cultural resources upon which teaching must draw. But it includes, too, members of the community, including employers, who quite rightly question the relevance of those resources to the economic and social world in which young people need to earn a living and find a quality of life. Above all, it includes teachers who mediate the inherited culture to the personal aspirations and needs of young people – who ensure that whatever the differences in cleverness or good fortune or background amongst those young people, their common humanity is recognised and their capacity 'to become human' is enhanced.
>
> (Pring 1995a)

NOTE

1 Laura Cumming described *Miss Smilla's Feeling for Snow* (Hoeg 1994) in a review as presenting a picture of a Denmark that is 'complacent and racist, susceptible to drug dealers, neo-Nazis and a bureaucracy so bent it could be folded into the pin-striped pocket of the sinister Cryolite Corporation.'

four

International comparisons

INTRODUCTION

It has become fashionable to compare educational statistics provided for the UK and other 'competitor' countries. We know, for instance, that the UK remains at the bottom end of the league table for participation rates in continuing and higher education, as compared with its international industrial partners. While Germany, France, Japan, the USA, The Netherlands and the Scandinavian countries manage a rate of 80 per cent or more, Britain still hovers around the figure of 50 per cent overall, slightly less than New Zealand and Australia (Richardson *et al.* 1995).

With regard to attainments in mathematics and science there have been a number of cross-national studies which suggest that Britain compares badly with almost everywhere else. At the end of June 1996, drawing on David Reynolds's and Shaun Farrell's research (Reynolds and Farrell 1996), *Panorama* highlighted the apparently remarkable differences in mathematical achievement between Taiwanese and English school children, implying that much of this was down to teaching styles (BBC 1996). According to a National Institute of Economic and Social Research (NIESR) study earlier that year, English 10-year-olds were two years behind their German and Swiss counterparts in terms of mental arithmetic, despite having been at school 18 months longer on average (Bierhoff 1996). Previous research by Sig Prais and Keith Wagner had shown that the average 14-year-old in France, Germany, Switzerland and The Netherlands was a year ahead in mathematics (Rafferty 1996). In 1991 Christopher Ball reported that 'on average British children are two years behind the Japanese in terms of basic mathematical competence' (Ball 1991). The Engineering Council (1993) claimed that British students were underachieving in comparison with those of other countries: only 27 per cent gaining GCSE grades A–C in the core subjects of English, mathematics and science, compared with 60 per cent in equivalent subjects in France and 62 per cent in Germany.

We need to be careful in interpreting such figures, of course. For example, it may be that more emphasis is placed in the UK upon aspects of mathematics such as geometry, which do not enter into the comparisons. There is clearly cause for concern though with regard to achievement levels, as the National Commission highlighted in 1993, with its survey of the percentage of young people gaining a comparable upper secondary school qualification, equivalent to our A level or GNVQ, at 18 (Japan 80 per cent, Germany 68 per cent, France 48 per cent, UK 29 per cent).

One response (as with the Reynolds and Farrell comparison with Taiwan noted above) is to blame British teachers (again) for being ineffective, with their woolly 1960s commitment to child-centred approaches. However, to claim that low ratings in international comparisons of standards of academic attainment are down to poor teaching is to ignore some fundamental questions, as Tony Tween, a primary school headteacher, pointed out in the *Times Educational Supplement* in 1996.

> What primary school teachers need now is not more mud slung from whatever source, but a clear view of what methods are most effective in what contexts. If we are to look across the Channel and to the Far East for (apparently) more effective teaching, we need to know whether, for example, those teachers have the same pastoral responsibilities, are effective with mixed-age classes, have a very broad curriculum to teach, work longer hours with bigger classes, or have the same obligations to report, record and consult as in this country.

Tony Tween could have added that comparisons of country by country spending *priorities* might also offer some explanations for apparent underperformance in British schools. An OECD survey of public expenditure as a proportion of GDP showed that the UK spends 4 per cent on state educational provision, while in countries like Hungary, Canada and Sweden the figure is higher than 7 per cent. Almost every other country in the OECD spends significantly more than the United Kingdom (OECD 1995; Cranford 1996). This reflects different priorities stemming from different value systems in respective countries. In some nation states, for example, military spending is seen as more important that spending on public services (Pilger 1996).

Even within 'this country', of course, there are some startling differences. The systems in Scotland and Northern Ireland are as different from that in England and Wales as they are from each other, and conditions of service reveal some interesting disparities. In Scotland, for instance, at the same time as their English counterparts were accepting the imposed settlement through the Teachers Pay and Conditions Act in 1987, Scottish teachers secured a deal that established $23\frac{1}{2}$ hours of class contact for secondary teachers, and maximum class sizes of 25 pupils. Although the concept of a General Teaching Council for teachers in England and Wales is still being debated, such a body has already existed in Scotland for more than thirty years. In Northern Ireland the grammar and secondary modern school system predominates, alongside an 11 plus examination, with very few independent schools.

With regard to the UK, the popular view is that the Scots have a very good system of education, having had universal state funded provision for much longer than south of the border. The general level of parental support for education is high, alongside an overall commitment to the comprehensive ethos. How does student attainment compare?

The level reached (by the end of secondary schooling) tends to be lower than in other European countries and in other parts of the United Kingdom. There has always been a belief in Scotland that breadth compensated for depth. This is not necessarily reflected in student attainment. A third of fifth year students pass no higher grade examinations and more than half get no more than one Higher. If four or five Higher passes in fifth year is regarded as a broad attainment, it is reached by only 20 per cent. It is found that many students do not develop good study skills at school and are poorly prepared for the rigours of a degree course.

(Murdoch and Dunning 1993)

But, as Tony Tween says above, are we comparing like with like in any of these comparisons? Such questions have bedevilled any attempts to draw lessons from comparative studies. International statistics that demonstrate the UK is 'underperforming' will always (and rightly) be greeted with scepticism, particularly where the yardstick is academic attainment. Most of us know, only too well, that the expectations on teachers and schools in the UK may be very different from those of our European, American or Far Eastern counterparts. The social, cultural and political contexts have to be taken into account, alongside a consideration of underpinning values.

VALUES AND THE DANISH CONTEXT

Chapter 3 noted that the values underpinning the education system in Denmark are different in some fundamental respects from those in the UK. The Danes make much of 'Jante's Law', which is concerned with the celebration of collective as opposed to individual achievement. If a pupil is more capable at doing maths than another it is her responsibility to help other pupils reach the same level. As with tulips in a Dutch bulb field, celebrating your ability to stand head and shoulders above others is not universally admired. Young people are not encouraged to gain purchase and self-esteem at the expense of others. The value base is one that is inclusive and has regard for the wider social and cultural context, where respect for others and consensus politics are both encouraged.

In asking whether Danish teachers and Danish schools are effective, we need to be clear about the yardsticks that operate in the Danish context. Student teachers from UWE who visit and study the Danish system are struck by the high level of resource provision, the informality and the small size of classes (White and Drower 1993). At the same time, they are critical of what they describe as rather traditional teaching. There is much whole class instruction, with pupils sitting at desks that face the blackboard; group work activities seem much less commonplace than in UK schools. Sometimes they even describe it as 'boring'. And it is certainly true that the level of noise, the heightened sense of activity, the cut and thrust between teacher and class is much less evident in Danish classrooms.

What do the Danes themselves say about their system? Interviews with a cross-section of people for a study into the significance of the affective domain in Danish education (White 1994) elicited the following comments:

Personal development is the key.

(Headteacher of a folk school)

What is most important for children is learning how to get on with each other and accept differences.

(Chairperson of a school board)

If you don't meet people with an opinion, you can't form your own.

(Headteacher of a free school)

Just because you're better than another pupil at maths or Danish or whatever doesn't mean you're a better person.

(16-year-old pupil in a folk school)

Most importantly, I want them to want to be here.

(Class teacher of a group of 8-year-olds)

Students need to consider what has gone into the two million years of production that have resulted in human beings.

(Head of a folk high school)

Here what you feel matters as much as what you think.

(13-year-old pupil in a free school)

The overall aim is to enable all our pupils to play an active part in society when they leave school and achieve fulfilment as individuals.

(Director of education for one *kommune*)

What is being emphasized here is the importance of the *affective* factors. This is not to say that the Danes disregard the *cognitive* but that they see the former as needing nurturing as a precursor for the latter. So pre-school provision is organized around cooperative play and practical activity. Learning through doing is a central feature of nursery schools and kindergartens. Reading and writing are not specifically encouraged in the early years and formal teaching in these areas only begins at 7. 'That way we ensure that all the children are ready to start. If you do it when they are five, some will be hopeless and fall way behind' (Folk high school class teacher). There is enough in Piagetian theory to support this view that until children have passed through the pre-operational phase (between 4 and 7 according to Piaget) they will not be able to manipulate symbols (Ginsberg and Opper 1969). Similarly, Bruner's view about how children pass through modes of representation, from the enactive to the iconic to the symbolic, provides additional theoretical support for the practical approach that is demonstrated in Danish kindergartens (Bruner 1960, 1966, 1986).

This decision to start compulsory schooling (and the teaching of reading) at 7 *may be* a very important factor in determining Danish children's subsequent attitudes to school (and society). And it is interesting to compare this with the situation in the UK, where there are strong pressures (often from parents) to get children into infant school and working on the 'basics' as soon as possible. British parents can become quite anxious if a child is not reading by the end of its first term in reception class. Comparisons start to be made with other children; anxieties mount; discussions take place about whether 'extra help' might be appropriate. There are clear expectations about performance in reading and writing.

Although there are many voices raised in opposition to this practice, for very good social and educational reasons, they are never taken seriously by policy makers. *Start Right* (Ball 1993), for example, was pilloried for daring to suggest that children should start formal schooling at 6, in line with every other EU country. 'An absurd recommendation' was how John Major described it. Yet the Danes have been practising this for many decades, and more than 90 per cent of their 16-year-olds *choose* to continue with further education at the point they leave secondary school, compared to a figure for the UK of 71 per cent (DfEE News 168/95).

And when they start 'proper school' at 6 or 7, the significance of the individual children within the class is celebrated and sustained. The class will be together with the same teacher for seven or eight years. It is important that they 'get on' with the teacher and with each other – that they come to respect and appreciate difference as well as similarity. The day is structured to support this process. Regular break times (ten minutes every hour) and a tradition of sharing food as a group within the classroom illustrate the importance attached to such dynamics. There are no extensive lunch breaks that are a feature of nearly every British primary and secondary school. Children are free to stay in the classrooms or go outside. The responsibility for looking after the room is shared with the class teacher. 'If we want children to care for society, they must care for each other' (Class teacher in a folk school). And Danish people generally *do* care for society. Twenty-one per cent of them are members of an environmental protection or conservation group, compared to 8 per cent in the UK (Eurostat 1991).

I have already referred to 'Jante's Law' and the widespread belief among school teachers and pupils that 'being better' than other pupils at school work does not mean you're a 'better' person. The tulip field analogy describes it very well. Critics might argue that this would encourage a sort of grey mediocrity, but in the Danish system the emphasis is different. There is no national testing before 16 and no attempt to produce league tables for school performance. The aim of the education system is to:

> give pupils the possibility of acquiring knowledge, skills, working methods and ways of expressing themselves which will contribute to the all round development of the individual pupils.
>
> (Danish Ministry of Education 1976)

Individual local authorities and schools are left to interpret how they go about this, within a national curriculum framework that sets the aims and objectives for individual subjects. This means that schools have extensive autonomy with regard to the planning of curricula and teaching methods. Teachers have a high status and level of respect among the communities that the schools serve, and many schools actively involve parents in the process of curriculum design.

> It is clear that, in comparison with many other countries, Danish parents possess an unusual degree of power in the school. To a foreign eye, unaccustomed to such prominence of parents in the school system, it might appear that the power of the professionals within the education system must thereby be very weak and their status low. That is not so. Because there is a powerful spirit of co-operation and consultation between parents, professionals and politicians, the system works with remarkable smoothness and lack of conflict.
>
> (Gronsved 1986)

Education is highly valued and funded accordingly. Teachers have very good working conditions, the sort of class sizes that would make most teachers in the UK blink in amazement, and complete control over *how* they teach (not 'deliver') their subjects in accordance with the overall aims and objectives of the ministry, and the curriculum focus agreed with the parents. Personal development is seen as central to the whole process. Relationships *between* staff and pupils, *among* the pupils and *with* the parents are highly regarded. Time is set aside for social and cultural activities that involve the whole class, including a residential trip *each year* that involves every pupil (and many parents as assistants).

The emphasis on affective factors is very evident in the whole process of schooling, and at every stage from kindergarten through to post-16 provision. The origins of this have been attributed to Nikolai Grundtvig, a nineteenth-century clergyman, and the founding father of the internationally renowned 'folk high school' movement. How one person's beliefs could actually influence a whole country's education system is a story in its own right, and one which many other writers have explored very fully (Jones 1970; Thaning 1982; Thodberg and Thyssen 1983; Bell 1988; Bjerg 1991; Andresen 1992). Grundtvig's fundamental belief was that *oplysning* (enlightenment) depended far more on the *levende ord* (the living word) than on classical education, which he considered too bookish. He wanted more attention to discussion, through what he described as the 'historic-poetic' method of teaching.

> Without the spoken word, life was dead. Down through the ages, the living word had been the very breath of history – without it there would have been no history. All books would have been dead, had they not been based on the spoken word.
>
> (Grundtvig quoted in Thaning 1982).

Grundtvig stressed the importance of *folkelighed* – education that was concerned with Danish culture and the Danish way of life. Interestingly, some of his inspiration came from visits he made to Cambridge University in the 1830s, where he noted the significance of the tutorial system and the amount of learning that took place in unstructured situations. His belief in the importance of the oral tradition found voice in his celebration of Nordic mythology. His ideas emerged at a point of national low ebb for Denmark. Defeat in various wars by their Prussian neighbours had reduced the size of the country and their self-esteem. Grundtvig argued that Danes needed to understand their 'Danishness' – rooted as it was in Scandinavian myths and legends – and take pride in the antiquity of their cultural roots. The folk high school movement in the latter half of the nineteenth century was a response to this.

> The most fundamental question behind the start of the Folk High School in the last century was not what should happen with the individual, but what should become of the Danish people. Where were they going, what was their relationship to their own past, how would they manage the challenges facing them?
>
> (Principal of Ry folk high school)

The collective concern nourished a reciprocal concern for individual development.

> We have learnt that no true self knowledge is possible without a critical analysis of both the individual and collective consciousness. A human being isn't just what he himself thinks he is. His consciousness is formed by both upbringing and social milieu. He must learn to look at himself in relation to these factors if he, in any truthful way, is to know himself and take responsibility for his existence. It is my belief that this critical analysis must be included in the curriculum of a Folk High School.
>
> (Andresen 1992)

The impact of Grundtvig's philosophy extended far beyond the boundaries of the folk high school. His influence in the formation of the underlying principles of universal Danish education are both acknowledged by the ministry and visible in official policy documents. The Folkeskole Act of 1975 (the equivalent of the UK's 1988 Education Act) requires the comprehensive system to:

> prepare pupils for taking an active interest in their environment and for participation in decision making in a democratic society, and for sharing responsibility for the solution of common problems. This, teaching and the entire daily life of the school must be based on intellectual freedom and democracy.
>
> (Danish Ministry of Education and Research 1992)

In the UK context it would be rather like the DfEE acknowledging the contribution that A. S. Neill of Summerhill fame had made to the notion of 'freedom' in British schools, and the curriculum consequences that flowed from it. It is very hard to conceive of such a possibility, since our own system can't point to a similar kind of originating force. But the Danish example demonstrates the power of the individual teacher to transform a society; and in that sense it offers inspiration to teachers everywhere who have a commitment to intellectual and individual freedom.

Grundtvig's beliefs in the importance of feelings, of creativity, of spirituality, of physical activity and of social and political responsibility bear a striking resemblance to many of the HMI 'areas of experience' that were put forward in the UK in 1977, where the recognition for the value of the affective as well as the cognitive was very present. And, interestingly, there is plenty of evidence that those schools which place significance on interpersonal relationships are also those schools where 'results' are good. Michael Rutter's work, for instance, highlighted the significance of residential activities in the development of a 'positive ethos'.

> We obtained very few measures of the extent of shared activity between staff and pupils, but it was found that schools in which a high proportion of children had been on out-of-school outings had better academic outcomes . . . shared activities towards a common goal which requires people to work together are a most effective means of reducing intergroup conflict.
>
> (Rutter *et al.* 1979)

It is interesting to reflect that the Manpower Services Commission also regarded 'residential experience' as a critical (and compulsory) component of the early Youth Opportunities Programme and its successor, the Youth Training Scheme, in the late seventies and early eighties (MSC 1981).

What is strange in the UK context is that we have enough evidence now to demonstrate the significance to learning of affective factors – that most of us acquire knowledge and skills in a manner that is more influenced by the context in which we learn, or by our feelings at the time, or by our ability to relate what is being learnt to previous experiences, than by how carefully the teacher constructs a linear progression through the syllabus (Kolb 1984; Abbott 1993; Donaldson 1993).

We have all experienced ourselves and witnessed in students enough 'ah-ha' experiences – those sudden flashes of insight so richly explored and described by Bronowski (1973) in that fine series *The Ascent of Man* and Koestler (1970) in *The Act of Creation* – to *know* that the trigger for this is very often a random event. What can transform the experience into some longer lasting and deeper understanding is the intervention of a skilled adult, and the opportunity for further reflection.

The idea that learning is a matter of challenges to and reformulation of personal theories or personal constructs, and that the role of the teacher is to lubricate these processes, is at the heart of many humanist approaches to learning. The writings of John Dewey (1916), R. F. Mackenzie (1970), Rudolf Steiner (1971), Carl Rogers (1983) and many others offer plenty of anecdotal evidence to support this view. 'The curriculum is the fig leaf that hides what's important. The most critical dynamic in school is what goes on between one pair of blue eyes and another.'[1]

BROADENING THE PERSPECTIVE: THE EUROPEAN UNION

For a *descriptive* account of the education systems in the various EU countries, the best document is that produced by the Education Information

Network in the European Community, which provides detailed information about the structures of the education and initial training systems in all the member states (Eurydice 1991). It states very clearly that 'no attempt to compare or evaluate the systems has been made', but the data in the document provide the basis for some interesting discussions about comparative provision. There are some fascinating differences, such as the length of compulsory schooling (until the age of 18 in Belgium), the extent of nursery provision (universal in Scandinavia), the wearing of school uniform (commonplace in the UK), the administrative structures (devolved to the autonomous regions in Spain), the control of curriculum matters (each *Land* in Germany) and the financing of education (1.7 per cent of GDP in The Netherlands).

For *comparison and evaluation* I found Penelope Weston and Robert Stradling's (1993) chapter in Harry Tomlinson's book *Education and Training 14–19* illuminating, alongside the series of books that constitutes Block 7, 'Education in Europe', of the Open University course EU 208 (1995), and would strongly recommend both of these perspectives, if you're interested in pursuing this further.

What Weston and Stradling point out is that those concerned with 14–19 provision in the EU member states have had to confront a number of common questions: how to achieve higher participation rates in post compulsory education and training; how to develop a better qualified workforce; how to enhance equality of opportunity; how to design a curriculum appropriate to the 21st century; how to measure the effectiveness of the respective system. In analysing how various countries have responded to these challenges they highlight that:

A basic principle of curriculum development and planning, formulated and reiterated in countless evaluation reports throughout western Europe, the United States and most of the English speaking world in the 1970s, has been ignored by several governments in the 1980s and early 1990s. That is, that time, resources and appropriate in-service training need to be given to build a consensus in support of the proposed changes; that teachers need to be actively involved in the curriculum development process and encouraged to 'own' the innovation; that changes need to be piloted, evaluated and revised where necessary and that the innovations need to be adequately resourced.

(Weston and Stradling 1993)

They contrast the four-month consultation period for the national curriculum in the UK (including the summer holiday period) with that in Spain, where the Ministry of Education in Madrid published its proposals for curriculum reform on the basis of an extensive period of piloting and evaluation that preceded the White Paper, and then allowed a further three years for consultation and debate before enacting the legislation.

This is not the only example where the UK seems to be out of step with its European partners. The trend in most education systems is away from detailed national programmes of study and towards less specific syllabuses that identify the broad topics to be covered, but not the detailed content.

Alongside this there is a growing recognition that effective curriculum change needs to be incremental, building on existing practice, rather than imposing radically dramatic changes.

Their conclusion highlights two further points of comparison which may have implications for developments in the UK. The first is that some of the assumptions underpinning the National Curriculum in England and Wales (such as the sequence of learning appropriate to ensure progression and continuity) are not substantiated by practices in other countries. The second is that although most European systems promote the notion of 'active learning', the practice in classrooms is very different because of resource constraints and teacher education.

> The particular context here – the 14–19 curriculum across the European spectrum – highlights the role of teachers and learners in shaping and changing the curriculum. The focus is increasingly on change in the process of learning, the most difficult kind to implement. This will require a sustained input of professional development. Perhaps the message then should be that we need to put more effort into making teachers and learners more competent in developing and structuring the learning process, in order to achieve common and individual curriculum goals within a complex and constrained system.
>
> (Weston and Stradling 1993)

THE 'NEW EUROPE'

How about those countries which have recently emerged from the domination of the Soviet system? How are curriculum priorities being redefined, and what is the role played by teachers?

The University of the West of England's Faculty of Education was the coordinating institution for one of the first EU-funded TEMPUS projects in Hungary and has subsequently been involved with similarly funded projects in Latvia and Albania. The principal focus of all these projects has been curriculum restructuring, and the experience has provided all of us involved with some rich insights into the evolution of national systems.

Although all are classed as 'formerly socialist' countries, the differences between the three were more noticeable than the similarities. As a Warsaw Pact country, Hungary was a quasi-autonomous state within the Soviet bloc, and one of the more affluent communist countries, with many links with Western Europe. Latvia was simply regarded as a region within the Soviet Union until its independence in 1991, with a Soviet dominated social, political and educational structure that had done its best to eradicate Latvian culture and language. Albania was an autonomous republic, which had severed all links with former allies such as the Soviet Union and China, and whose leader Enver Hoxha maintained a self-imposed policy of almost total isolation from the rest of the world.

Following democratic reforms in the early 1990s, all three countries had to confront a number of major problems, some of which were shared with the other 'socialist' countries of Central and Eastern Europe. Pressures to modernize the curriculum were constrained by organizational inflexibility, lack of suitably trained staff and available resources. For example, in their desire to replace Russian as the compulsory second language (or, in the case of Latvia, to replace Russian as the *main* language) and extend the teaching of English in particular, all these ex-socialist countries have encountered enormous problems associated with supply and demand. Many of the good teachers of English that existed at the point of transition were courted by the world of business and commerce, eager to develop trading relationships with Western Europe. Salaries on offer in the commercial sector were many times higher than those guaranteed by the state. It was not surprising that many English teachers left their posts in schools, and replacing them has been a major challenge facing respective ministries of education. Multiply this challenge by the number of curriculum subjects that needed updating (such as information technology), and you have some idea of the problem. Add to that the desire to modernize the prevailing pedagogies, and you can see that each of these countries was confronted by a Herculean task.

The TEMPUS programme was initiated by the European Union in part to address this problem: to offer funds for renewal and updating of curriculum and pedagogies in university departments. Some of that filtered through to Faculties of Education and Teacher Training Colleges, where curriculum issues and teaching methods were considered priority areas (Eliot 1996). In Hungary the programme was concerned with the teaching of English and the development of curriculum materials for primary school teachers to use in encouraging 'personal autonomy' among their pupils. In Latvia it was English again, the development of curriculum materials for the teaching of citizenship and environmental education (Clough and Menter 1995) and teaching methods. In Albania, the focus is on curriculum issues (such as English, special education, environmental education) and organizational restructuring.

We have been aware from the start of each of these projects that we have much to learn as well as to share. The developments have been two-way for all parties involved. Those who might write off the soviet style schooling model for its didactic and autocratic pedgagogy need to reflect on some of its successes, like the capability of its students to take in information in a lecture style situation. The level of fluency of Hungarians, Latvians and Albanians in English was quite remarkable – particularly in the latter two countries, where contact with 'foreigners' had been dangerous folly, and tuning in to the BBC World Service a punishable offence.

Literature related to curriculum developments and professional matters in the countries of Central and Eastern Europe is beginning to enter educational journals and bookshelves, although there is precious little written that offers the sort of broad overview of the kind presented by Eurydice (the Education Information Network in the European Community). For an analysis of issues surrounding curriculum development in the context of national restructuring, with particular reference to Latvia, Albania, Hungary, Bulgaria and Slovakia, see Menter and White (1997).

THE UNITED STATES OF AMERICA

The United States is experiencing many of the same problems that confront policy makers in the UK. There is concern over international comparisons that rank student achievement on a par with the UK, the 'drop out' rate (as opposed to our description of 'school leaving' rate) is 25 per cent, functional illiteracy is at an alarming level and public confidence in schools is reckoned to be at an all time low.

Inevitably there have been a series of policy papers and discussions at national level about the notion of a national curriculum, such as that launched by the President in 1992 called United Sates 2000, which specified studies in six core areas: English, mathematics, science, languages, history and geography. Student achievement would be determined at years 4, 8 and 12, using a number of achievement levels that bear some similarity to the UK national curriculum (Paulter 1993).

In an article entitled 'Should America have a national curriculum?' Elliot Eisner considers a number of issues that have a bearing on any answer, including: the tradition of state and local control in a context of wide cultural diversity, which challenges the notion of a universal curriculum remote-controlled from the White House; the inability of the profession to assess what matters and provide a telling picture of the strengths and weaknesses of schools; and the focus on symptoms at the expense of structural issues.

> What is even more troublesome is that almost all of the national proclamations for school reform, including those demanding higher standards and tougher courses, neglect the deeper mission of schooling: the stimulation of curiosity, the cultivation of intellect, the refinement of sensibilities, the growth of imagination, and the desire to use these unique and special human potentialities . . . This neglect of the deeper mission of schooling is paralleled only by the unwillingness to address the complex, systemic features of schooling, especially what teachers need. The President's reform effort has paid virtually no attention to the school as an organization, as a workplace, as a slice of culture, as a community displaying a certain ethos, and as an array of intellectual and social norms.
>
> (Eisner 1991)

Eisner identifies 'five dimensions' that America cannot afford to neglect: the intentional, the structural, the curricular, the pedagogical and the evaluative. It is a list which finds echoes in the debates and discussions about curricular innovation in the UK, and one which begs fundamental questions about the aims of schooling and the values that underpin any answers.

Although there is no national curriculum as yet, there is congressional concern that there should be some nationally coordinated programmes to improve standards in the nation's 110,000 schools. At an invitational conference on the 'hidden consequences of the national curriculum' in June 1993, a number of contributors urged caution in applying a blanket reform policy that ignored local concerns and professional judgement. One of the contributors was Herbert Kliebard, whose writings on curriculum issues are internationally acclaimed (Kliebard 1986, for instance).

> Curriculum reform should be done in the interest of creating a truly enlightened citizenry, not in the interest of using educational reform as a surrogate for addressing questions of national interest directly. Using schools to meet economic or national needs that are not directly related to schooling is likely to be inconsequential for the problems that this practice was intended to resolve, save for the symbolic function of cuing the public that some kind of action has been taken to do something.
>
> (Eisner 1993)

Although the system is more decentralized than that in the UK – which is partly a product of the enormous size of the country – with 1600 school boards serving the 110,000 schools (compared with 25,000 in the UK) for the 47 million students across 50 states, the government is pushing ahead with proposals to create some sort of core curriculum.

In analysing the underlying belief systems that drive the American system, Gary Rhoades (1989) illustrates a number of important points of contrast with the UK. Inclusiveness is more apparent in the USA. Access to some kind of higher education is open to everyone; access to elite institutions is open to those who succeed in an aptitude test that measures 'general academic potential' and is criterion referenced. The consequence of this is a broadening of the school curriculum, a relaxation on modes of assessment and reporting, a blurring of the distinction between the academic and the vocational, between education and training that is such a strong feature still of the UK scene.

> English classes tend to focus as much on mechanics as on literature. Mathematics classes also concentrate on the repetition of basic skills, and social studies classes combine the classic topics of American history and government and are geared to civic and assimilation goals . . . American schools are more concerned with 'preparation for life' than preparation for college.
>
> (Rhoades 1989)

It would seem that, in contrast to the curriculum in the UK, the one in American schools is designed to address the interests of students and society and operates on a principle of inclusivity rather than exclusivity. Rhoades refers to Pierre Bourdieu's concept of 'cultural capital' (Bourdieu 1974), which he considers is used as a basis for exclusion in the UK, where what is valued by the education establishment is a particular sort of 'elite' culture that is very different from the 'common' culture. In the USA there are calls for 'cultural literacy' from conservatives as well as liberals.

> For example, Hirsch (1987) proposed a curricular core that covers material 'every American needs to know in order to participate meaningfully in the cultural and civic community'. Moreover, he proposes to make a major part of the hidden curriculum explicit, to have the schools teach cultural knowledge and enhance students' cultural capital, so that all will

have access to it. The express aim is not the selecting and grooming of the few, but the inculcating and inclusion of the many.

(Rhoades 1989)

In part this can be traced back to the historical evolution of the public secondary school sector in America, which was much less dominated by the private school and university interest groups than has been the case in the UK, where the comprehensive curriculum was based on the grammar school curriculum of the 1950s, which in turn drew on the traditions of the endowed Elizabethan schools and the prestigious public schools. When dominated by a public model that links secondary education to elementary education, it is more likely to provide general experience and education that prepares students for a wide variety of life activity. The American curriculum model reflects parental concerns that place 'personal and vocational' goals on a par with 'intellectual' goals (Goodlad 1984), in sharp contrast to the UK, where parental concern focuses on the maintenance of standards and the provision of academic curricular and exam structures that will enhance their children's access to universities.

As indicated in Chapter 3, a central issue seems to be that of values, with discussions about policy and practice in the American context influenced by a concern for 'client interest', while in the UK the concern is about standards and selection.

AUSTRALIA AND NEW ZEALAND

Gary Rhoades extends his cross-national comparison of conceptions of the curriculum to include Australia, which he demonstrates has much more in common with the UK than with the USA. Historically the Australian and New Zealand education systems have been much influenced by Britain, recruiting teachers from UK schools in large numbers right up to the end of the 1970s. Student enrolment in private schools is around twice the level for the UK, but the essentials of the state-funded sector remain much the same. The Higher School Certificate is the Australian equivalent of A level, and the standard against which all else is measured (Rhoades 1989). However, one of the interesting developments in Australia is the reduced reliance on these exams and the experimentation with other testing technologies. In Queensland, for instance, external examinations were abandoned in the 1970s, and other states have changed to a system where up to 50 per cent of a student's final mark is derived from school-based assessment (Mackinnon 1988).

Both New Zealand and Australia have experienced similar challenges of rising unemployment, and a perceived mismatch between educational objectives and economic performance (McKinnon et al. 1991). As Philip Hughes pointed out in a paper to an OECD conference on Education in Asia and the Pacific in 1994 (Hughes 1992, 1994), Australia and New Zealand have been moving in the same direction as the UK in terms of curricular reform.

New Zealand requires individual schools to manage their own affairs, including finances, in the framework of a national curriculum specifying seven learning areas: Language (which includes English), Mathematics, Science and the Environment, Society and Culture, Art, Physical Education and Personal Development, and Technology. The legislation also defines six areas of Essential Skills: Communication, Numeracy, Information handling, Social, Problem-solving and Decision making; and Work and Study. The expectation is that student achievement will be defined and reported at ten levels.

(Hughes 1994)

The Australian picture is rather similar, although there are many initiatives still unresolved.

The Australian Education Council (AEC) reached agreement in 1989 on ten common and agreed goals (the Hobart Declaration). This included the specification of eight common areas of learning as a basis for a national approach to curriculum: English, Mathematics, Science, Languages, Society and Environment, Arts, Health, and Technology. A national agency, the Curriculum Corporation, has been established to carry out curriculum mapping, i.e. description of the current curriculum situation throughout Australia. Following the mapping, the Curriculum Corporation has begun to develop curriculum framework statements, initially in English, Mathematics and Science. Assessment of students will occur through national profiles, using eight achievement levels in knowledge, skills and understanding.

(Hughes 1994)

Hughes highlights three reports by Finn (1991), Mayer (1992) and Carmichael (1992) which have influenced curriculum responses to the changing social and economic circumstances in Australia; the first setting a target of 90 per cent of students completing year 12 by the year 2001 and demonstrating competence in six key areas (language and communication, mathematics, scientific and technological understanding, cultural understanding, problem solving, and personal and interpersonal); the second, expressing the interests of business and industry, reducing Finn's key areas of competencies to a more restrictive and work related list; and the Carmichael report providing the vocational framework in which these key areas of competency can be achieved and demonstrated.

The conflicts within the Australian system mirror many of those in the UK, with teachers often opposed to the 'instrumentalist' views of government ministers, employers and vocational trainers, who make direct links between the state of the economy and the performance of schools. As in Britain, many *educators* look on unemployment as a product of technological and economic change, not indicative of any failure of the school system. However effectively they prepare students for the world of work, if there are not enough jobs to go round, they will, at best, have produced a better educated group of unemployed people. There is great resistance to the suggestion that schools are failing, since there is plenty of evidence (as in the UK) that more students are reaching higher standards in broader areas of achievement than at any other time in history.

Interestingly, given that the ASDAN Award Scheme is the major case study of successful curriculum innovation in this book, it is worth noting the interest being expressed by Australian educators in devising programmes that acknowledge a much broader profile of student achievement (Kramer 1991). It is also worth noting that Australia mirrors some aspects of the USA, with its devolution of responsibility to the respective state governments. An interesting examination of the relationship between curriculum reform at state level and the nationally determined priorities (as set out by the Hobart Declaration, for example) is provided by David Carter in an article 'Structural change and curriculum reform in an Australian education system' (1993).

THE PACIFIC RIM

The economic 'miracle' of many of the pacific rim countries provides rich opportunities for politicians and mounds of copy for journalists to make comparisons between their education systems and those of the UK. While the 'growth rate' of many of these countries is in double figures, the UK figure stands at an optimistic forecast of 2 per cent. It is often suggested that if only we could emulate aspects of their school system, we might emulate their economic performance. The *Worlds Apart* report referred to on page 39 (Reynolds and Farrell 1996) generated such a response.

However, returning to the point Tony Tween was making at the beginning, we need to be clearer whether we are comparing like with like in notions about 'effective teaching'. Are the same expectations that are placed on teachers in the UK being placed on teachers in those countries referred to as the Asian Tigers? Do the social and political structures merit some comparisons too? The issue of values comes to the surface yet again.

For a description and analysis of the education systems and curriculum concerns in these countries, a very good source is the OECD report referred to above. This was the outcome of an international conference held in Hiroshima in 1992, which brought together representatives from the OECD and what were referred to as the dynamic Asian economies (DAEs) of Hong Kong, Malaysia, South Korea, Taiwan, Thailand and Singapore. The focus was on the current educational trends and curricular concerns in the participating countries (OECD 1994).

CONCLUSION

The danger with any analysis of curriculum innovation that relies on academic publications, conference reports and policy pronouncements by government ministers is that it *may* well overlook what is actually happening in the classroom. It can't be presumed that national *policy* is necessarily reflected in school *practice* (Berg 1992). To do so would be like making assumptions about what is going on in UK classrooms on the basis of such government publications as *Better Schools* (DES 1985), *Education and Training for the 21st Century* (DES 1991) and the DfEE's list of approved qualifications.

Children's television series such as *Grange Hill* and the numerous articles by teachers writing on curriculum issues in the *Times Educational Supplement* (like those reproduced in Chapter 6) may provide a more realistic view of what is going on in UK schools.

I came across glimpses of the *actual* experience of teachers and students in a number of countries through a few of the papers that the library database scrolled up. 'The teaching of mathematics in a Massachusetts high school' (Eilerman and Stanley 1994), 'The construction of a mathematics curriculum for Queensland teachers' (Clatworthy and Galbraith 1991), 'Language aware-ness in Italian schools' (Balboni 1993), 'Technology education in Japan' (Okuya *et al.* 1993) and 'History teaching in the Danish folkeskole' (Nielsen 1991) were some examples from the thousands of entries associated with curric-ulum development.

All of these underline the point that teachers throughout the world are still operating at the heart of any curriculum innovation; that their ability to interpret and make sense of nationally determined curriculum priorities makes a significant difference; that teachers everywhere have the capacity to operate at what Tim Brighouse referred to as 'the golden cusp of the teacher's skill: his or her ability to open the mind' (Brighouse 1994).

NOTE

1 Quote from Emeritus Professor W. D. Wall's keynote speech at a conference at Bristol University School of Education in 1978 at the launch of *In and Out of School*.

five

The curriculum map

INTRODUCTION

Following the Dearing Reports of 1994 and 1996, there have been significant changes in the National Curriculum requirements for students of compulsory school age, as well as in the nature and provision of post-16 courses.

Pre-16, the mandatory requirements at Key Stage 4 have been limited to English, mathematics, single science, physical education and short courses in technology and a modern foreign language. Religious education and sex education remain as compulsory components. This 'slimline' version was intended to allow schools more scope for introducing a range of academic and vocational options. In practice though, many schools are finding it difficult to fit the compulsory element into 60 per cent, which further squeezes the time available for those subjects and activities which form the remaining 40 per cent. The humanities and expressive arts have been most affected. Although the notion of 'short courses' sounds attractive, it creates enormous timetabling and teaching problems. Personal and social education and careers guidance programmes, which are highly valued in many schools, are bound to be under threat in such circumstances. Talk of two hours of compulsory PE only exacerbates the problem.

Post-16, the removal of colleges of further education from LEA control, the commitment to certain National Training and Education Targets, the introduction of GNVQs and NVQs, the 'output related' nature of the funding of many courses, the introduction of Training Credits, the privatization of the Careers Service and the removal of 16- and 17-year-olds from the unemployment register have all combined to alter radically post-16 education and training in schools and colleges.

It seems helpful to consider these changes in qualifications and curriculum provision under three interrelated headings:

- the programmes on offer pre-16;
- the programmes on offer post-16;

• the assessment and accreditation arrangements associated with these programmes.

What follows in this chapter is a brief consideration of each of these aspects, which provides a useful 'map of the territory'.

Figure 5.1 gives a visual illustration of the various 'progression routes' that are now available to students.

PRE-16 PROGRAMMES

General Certificate of Secondary Education (GCSE)

In 1986 the GCE and CSE examinations were merged into a common exam for 16-year-olds. It is also possible for those aged 17 and over in full-time education to take the GCSE (mature) syllabus, and for those not in full-time education to take the GCSE (external) syllabus.

Grades are awarded on a scale of A to G, with moderation provided by one of six regional examination boards. Recently, however, City and Guilds and The Royal Society of Arts have entered the GCSE market, offering a range of technology and business studies awards, and it is possible for other organizations to compete in the 'free market' against the traditional exam boards. GCSEs are subject specific (e.g. maths, English, geography and so on), but the nature of the criterion-referenced assessment and the emphasis on process and problem solving skills meant a radical reappraisal of teaching strategies.

In GCSE terminology, each of the subject areas is divided into at least three domains (e.g. English is separated into oral communication, reading and writing; geography is separated into specific geographic knowledge, geographical understanding, map and graphic skills, and application of geography to economic, environmental, political and social issues). Within each domain, levels of performance are specified and candidates achieve points for demonstrations of competence. The points scored in each domain are aggregated to produce the final grade (A to G).

Although the GCSE was intended to cater for all pupils, concern has grown over the perceived validity of the lower grades. Job adverts indicate that some employers' perspectives have changed very little, and it is still not uncommon for some of these 'end users' to ask 'Which of the GCSE grades is equivalent to an O level pass?' The original notion presented by the Joint Council that grades G and F would be 'foundation grades from which all can build' has simply demonstrated the triumph of hope over experience. The introduction of 'half GCSEs' in 1996 was intended to broaden the uptake and success rate.

One of the stated aims of the introduction of GCSE was to raise standards, and the criterion referenced framework of assessment which marked students according to clearly spelt out levels of performance seemed to be a much fairer system than the norm referencing system of O levels (although there is some evidence to suggest this *may* not actually be the case, since markers are trained on the 'norms' of previous years). It was ironic that the national results of 1992, which showed a significant increase in the number

Figure 5.1 Diagram of the curriculum map

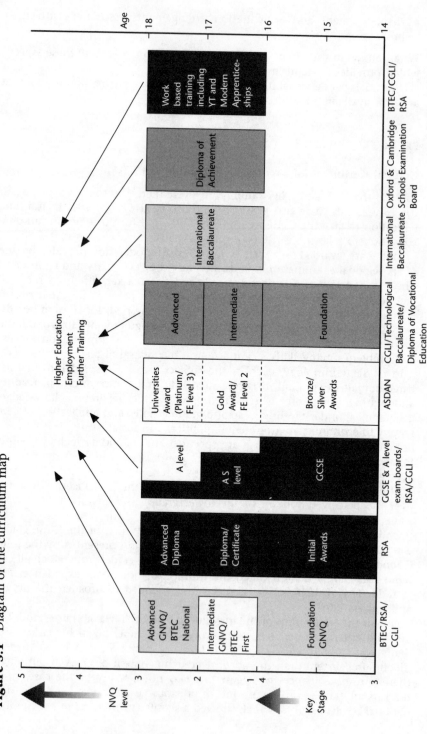

of pupils achieving high grades, should have been greeted by claims from the government that this was because teachers had lowered their standards in marking course work! The resulting order from the Secretary of State for Education (Kenneth Clarke) prohibited 100 per cent course work in English and reduced course work in all subjects, despite various surveys which concluded that standards had, in fact, risen across the board.[1] Many schools had to abandon some excellent Mode 3 GCSEs.

The 1988 report of the Task Group on Assessment and Testing, which established the framework of Key Stages with its ten levels of attainment, anticipated the possibility of phasing out GCSEs as the basis for assessment at 16. However, the ten level scale now only continues until the end of Key Stage 3, so that GCSE gradings have been retained for Key Stage 4 (although the reduction in the statutory core has affected the *number* of GCSE entries in many schools).

Probably more significant than the revamping of the compulsory core has been the whole issue of 'league tables' of GCSE results. Since 1994, schools have been required to furnish the DFEE with data relating to the percentage of year 11 pupils obtaining five or more GCSEs at grade C or above. Publication of these raw data in the national press has engendered considerable resentment – particularly among the 'losers' and those who consider the lack of reference to any 'value added' concepts an affront to fundamental egalitarian principles. Inevitably it has added to the pressure on schools – for 'poor' performers to do better and 'high' performers not to allow standards to slip. Evidence is emerging of schools taking calculated decisions to invest time of key staff in coaching those on the D/C grade borderline, at the expense of those well below or above the line.

Another issue in relation to GCSEs is the growing feeling among teachers that they are a 'gigantic irrelevance' (White and Brockington 1983). Since the percentage of young people staying on at 16 has risen to around 70 per cent, the issue of coherent 14–19 provision becomes more important than some arbitrary assessment at 16, which is no longer seen as a final exam. The National Union of Teachers' research referred to in Chapter 3 (NUT 1995b) highlighted the very real professional concern about the validity of retaining GCSEs in their current form.

The Diploma of Vocational Education (DOVE)

The Diploma of Vocational Education replaced the Joint BTEC/CGLI Foundation Programme and took on board many of the principles and practice espoused by this programme and the Certificate of Pre-vocational Education (CPVE), its associated post-16 initiative.

Accredited by the City and Guilds of London Institute (CGLI), the foundation level of the DOVE is intended for years 10 and 11. It was promoted as the principal 'alternative' course to the GCSE, although many schools that operate the ASDAN Award Scheme have adopted this framework in preference, since it embraces much of the Key Stage work already being taught, and encourages a cross-curricular approach.

The issue of whether the diploma would become part of a dual track system was critical to its development. CGLI insisted that the foundation level of the DOVE was appropriate for the entire ability range and that participating schools should run it accordingly, alongside GCSEs. However, the indications are that such courses are considered more appropriate for the 'lower ability' end of the range.

Foundation GNVQs

Since September 1994 the CGLI has also been accrediting Foundation GNVQs in art and design, business, health and social care, leisure and tourism, and manufacturing, as well as piloting courses in engineering, land based industries, distribution, information technology, and media and communication, some of which are available within Key Stage 4. Following the Dearing Review in 1996 schools were encouraged to develop these more widely, and it is now possible for 14-year-olds to transfer to colleges to undertake such vocational programmes.

In addition to Foundation GNVQs, City and Guilds also accredits a range of core skills and languages courses, which can be taken pre-16, such as Numberpower and Wordpower, as well as certain Pitman qualifications, such as word processing and understanding computers.

CGLI Technological Baccalaureate

The Technological Baccalaureate offers a course for students in the 14–18 age group who are interested in a technological career and want to progress into higher education in the UK or abroad, or go straight into employment. Following a three-year pilot phase, mainly in some CTCs and schools in Hereford and Worcester, and evaluation by London University, it was made widely available in September 1994.

Pre-16 it provides a flexible means of delivering the core curriculum and certain foundation subjects at Key Stage 4 (e.g. technology and modern language), as well as offering a framework for core (now 'key') skill assessment. Within the Technological Baccalaureate framework tutors have considerable freedom over the design of the programme. Students accumulate credit in certain 'units' which correspond to National Curriculum demands at Key Stage 4 and which count towards the three levels of award of the Technological Baccalaureate post-16 (see page 65).

Royal Society of Arts (RSA) awards

As well as GCSE qualifications in design and technology, business studies, information studies and information systems, students can take an RSA Certificate in Information Technology which covers Attainment Target 5 and associated programmes of study. RSA also offers joint accreditation with the Southern Examinations Group (SEG) for GCSEs in economics, statistics, information systems and keyboarding (the latter two being modular courses), and accredits initial awards in the following subject areas (agricultural studies, care, computer graphics, environmental studies, food technology, life skills, media studies, office studies, sports and recreation, textiles, travel and tourism), and a whole range of certificates in numeracy, mail merge, multi-media, shorthand speed test, spreadsheets, typewriting skills, word processing and so on.

London Chamber of Commerce and Industry Examinations Board

Like RSA and Pitman, LCCI provides accreditation for a plethora of office skills related courses such as audio transcription, book-keeping, commercial calculations, English for business, numberpower, secretarial studies and vocational access.

Other courses

In addition to the nationally organized awards mentioned above, there are a number of other programmes that schools offer the 14–16 age group, some of which run right through to 18 or beyond, including:

- Graded tests (often in modern languages and offered by almost every LEA in the country).
- Work related activities, such as Project Trident and Mini Enterprise, which focus on the work experience arrangements and links between schools and industry/commerce.
- Curriculum enrichment programmes such as the Liverpool University Enrichment Programme, Active Tutorial Work, CREST Awards and Somerset Thinking Skills.
- Programmes designed specifically for 'slow learners', such as the Welsh Certificate of Educational Achievement.
- Extra-curricular activities, such as the Duke of Edinburgh's Scheme, which offers awards at bronze, silver and gold level for demonstration of involvement and competence in a range of activities; and a whole range of awards for demonstration of competence in practical, physical and creative activities (such as the Royal Life Saving Society awards, the St John Ambulance Three Cross Award and Road Safety awards.

The ASDAN Youth/Universities Award Scheme

Originally conceived by a group of teachers who were concerned about the place of personal and social education in the curriculum, and drawing extensively on the 'good practice' of the Technical and Vocational Education Initiative (TVEI), with its emphasis on a more negotiated, modular and activity based curriculum, the Award Scheme has proved to be a most remarkable success story (see Chapter 8).

The Award Scheme Development and Accreditation Network (ASDAN), a not for profit organization linked to the Youth Education Service educational charity, and representing the consortia of participating establishments, manages the Youth/Universities Award Scheme, which straddles the pre-16 and post-16 experience, offering a progressive series of awards at bronze, silver, gold and platinum/universities levels. In addition, ASDAN accredits parallel programmes that have been specially designed for the FE sector and vocational training (the Further Education Award and Foundation Training Award respectively). This whole suite of awards provides a curriculum enrichment activity, as well as a way of assessing and accrediting key skill competence at NVQ related levels 1 to 4.

Curriculum materials, such as *Workright* and *Towards Independence*, are also available to support other programmes being specifically developed for special needs groups post-16.

The scheme's capacity to enrich the curriculum experience for sixth formers aiming at university entrance, and to provide evidence of key skill achievement across the whole 14–19 curriculum, as well as enabling those in the 'special needs' category to attain awards, goes part way to explaining its remarkable expansion throughout the UK. In addition, and perhaps equally important for staff, at a time when some feel their very professionalism is under critical scrutiny, it offers *classroom* teachers and lecturers the opportunity to draw on their own experience and judgement in designing and implementing the programme of activities.

POST-16 PROGRAMMES

In addition to the ASDAN Award Schemes, which are designed (as are GNVQs) to straddle the pre- and post-16 experience, the following are specifically intended for the post-16 age group.

Advanced and Advanced Supplementary (A and AS) levels

As the 'gold standard' of the English and Welsh education system, A levels still provide the principal access route to higher education. Until 1995, with the exception of programmes like the Wessex Modular course, A levels retained their traditional structure of a two-year course of study leading to a final exam. In that year, following the positive findings of the Wessex evaluation, SCAA agreed to approve certain modular syllabuses, which led to a rapid take up of such courses in maths, English, science, geography, business and economics. Graded on a scale of A to E, moderation is provided by one of the nine examination boards.

AS levels, introduced in 1986 and equivalent to half an A level, offer a one-year programme of study that is similar in design to A level and moderated by the same exam boards.

The *traditional* structure of A levels has come in for much criticism.

Although around one-third of each age cohort sits this final exam at 18 only two-thirds of these (i.e. 25 per cent of the age group) achieve the two or more A levels that are the minimum entrance qualification for admission to university (and then only 60 per cent of these actually gain a place). Of the remainder, there is some evidence to suggest that they are worse off after this extra two years of 'failed' study (particularly in terms of employment opportunities) than their counterparts who left school at 16. So not only do A levels disenfranchise large numbers of the cohort who take them, but they also ensure that the other two-thirds of young people who 'made do' with a mixture of vocational qualifications, training courses and limited job opportunities instead are seen as having taken the 'second best' option.

The Higginson Committee recommended a radical reform of A levels in 1988, arguing that the existing structure did not serve the interests of people who took the exam. Pressures for reform had been growing from below. The development of GCSE, with continuous assessment and innovative teaching methods, heightened the anachronistic nature of many A levels in the eyes of students and teachers, and this perception was shared by some in very senior educational positions, like Sir Edward Parkes, Vice Chancellor of Leeds University and Chairman of the then Committee of Vice Chancellors and Principals:

> A levels are the things which are a sore thumb in the whole system now – the sooner we get rid of them the better. I know that some people regard them as the firm rock in the shifting sands of educational change, but no Vice Chancellor wants them for a moment.
>
> (Parkes 1990)

One of the key proposals in the Higginson Report was to extend the number of subjects taken to five in an endeavour to bridge the traditional science and arts divide, and encourage students to go for breadth of subject experience, as young people do in Scotland with 'Highers'. Although the proposals were endorsed by many influential bodies (including the CBI, TUC and AUT), they were never implemented by the Conservative government. There was a publicly stated commitment, endorsed by the introduction of the 'starred' A level and the 1996 Dearing Review, to maintain and reinforce the 'rigour' of the 'gold standard', even though it has never been made clear what this absolute standard referred to actually is – given the wide spread of A levels courses. (How does an A in physics compare to an A in classics, for example?)

Dearing took the view that increasing the emphasis on process and skills within A levels, extending the option to combine academic and vocational courses, and reforming AS levels was enough change to broaden the experience of those on A level courses. This was not a view universally shared.

> Nothing could better demonstrate that the academic route to qualifications is to remain theoretical, pure and untainted by contact with the real world . . . By the end of this century the sixth form curriculum of public schools and a reintroduced selective system looks like being indistinguishable from that of 50 years ago.
>
> (Macfarlane 1996)

General National Vocational Qualifications (GNVQs)

GNVQs are awarded by BTEC, CGLI or RSA, and have replaced some of the pre-vocational courses (like BTEC First and National, RSA Diploma and Advanced Diploma, or CGLI Intermediate and Advanced Diploma) previously accredited by these bodies, although such courses are still much in evidence in colleges of further education. Their biggest impact has been in sixth forms, where schools have been able to offer 'vocational' courses for the first time.

Introduced in the White Paper *Education and Training for the 21st Century* (DES 1991), the GNVQ was intended to provide the principal full-time 'alternative' to A levels in schools and colleges, so as to enhance attainment levels and achieve the goals set in the National Training and Education Targets (NTETs) for the year 2000.

> We are aiming to establish three broad qualification pathways for our young people – the A level system, NVQs and the new GNVQs . . . which will stand alongside academic qualifications on their own merits. GNVQs will play a central role in our strategy for 16–19-year-olds. I want GNVQs in at least two subjects to be available in at least 1500 schools and colleges by 1996.
>
> (Kenneth Clarke 5 April 1993)

Achievement of a GNVQ at level 3 is stated to be equivalent to two A levels and sufficient for university entrance.

In September 1993 the first GNVQs were offered in five subject areas (art and design, business, health and social care, leisure and tourism, manufacturing). This was subsequently extended to include science, construction and the built environment, catering and hospitality, retail and distribution, engineering, information technology, management studies, media, communication and production, performing arts and entertainment industries, and land-based and environmental industries.

Level 3 (known as Advanced GNVQ and equivalent to BTEC National, CGLI Advanced Diploma or RSA Advanced Diploma) is awarded on completion of 12 GNVQ 'units' (plus the key skill units described below). There are eight mandatory units covering the principles, processes and skills common to a range of occupations within the broad vocational area, and four optional units chosen from a specified range. It is possible for 'more able' students to gain additional units (18 units are seen as equivalent to three A levels) or to undertake a 12-unit GNVQ at level 3 alongside two AS levels or one A level. The development of modular A levels has made it possible for students to combine GNVQs with A level studies, assuming 'co-teachability' can be organized in respective institutions.

Level 2 (known as Intermediate GNVQ and equivalent to BTEC First, CGLI Intermediate Diploma, or RSA Diploma) consists of four mandatory and two optional units. Level 1 (known as Foundation GNVQ and referred to on page 60 above), consists of three mandatory and three optional units.

As with other vocational courses, students progress by the regular completion of modules, providing a 'portfolio of evidence' for internal assessment, and sitting an externally moderated test. Students are able to resit this test until they reach the 80 per cent pass mark. An award of merit and distinction grades will be based on the overall quality of the work presented by the candidate.

GNVQs proved to be popular following the pilot phase in 1992/3. Some

82,000 students enrolled in the first year, rising to over 200,000 registrations by 1996. Enthusiasm for this course is high among students and staff. The workload can be daunting, however, requiring staff to handle hundreds of different test papers, and there is still concern over the status of GNVQs compared to the A level gold standard.

The restyling of GNVQs as 'applied' A levels under the common umbrella of 'National Advanced Diploma', as outlined in the Dearing Review, is intended to address the issue of parity of esteem. How much impact this will have on employers and higher education remains to be seen. The requirement of evidence of achievement in the 'key skills' (communication, application of number and information technology), for *all* courses accredited at the level of Advanced Diploma, may help in this respect, as these have always formed an essential ingredient of GNVQs under the heading of 'core skills'. Indeed, it is the *core* (now *key*) skills component of the GNVQs which comprise a large part of the 'G', in contrast to NVQs (see page 66 below) and A levels themselves, in which these skills do not feature at all prominently.

In a further effort to enhance parity of esteem with A levels, external assessments are to become 'more rigorous'. This may placate critics of GNVQs, like Alan Smithers (1993) with his description of GNVQs as 'a crisis of epic proportions', but it may turn out to be counterproductive in terms of progress towards the National Training and Education Targets (NTETs), as the rise in enrolment and achievement may falter. The added danger is that the 'voluntarism' of the Dearing Review will simply allow schools and colleges to continue promoting separate tracks, with those like the independent schools maintaining the view that GNVQs (or applied A levels) are for the 'less able' students (i.e. those doing anything less than three A levels).

> One of the problems we have had in this country for centuries is the sharp distinction between academic learning which is seen as relevant for the few, and vocational training which is seen as appropriate for the vast majority. I think this is a false dichotomy – that distinctions between that which is academically respectable and that which is vocationally relevant need to be questioned.
>
> (Pring 1996)

CGLI Technological Baccalaureate

Building on the units offered at Key Stage 4, the Technological Baccalaureate offers awards at three levels post-16: the foundation level, equivalent to the CGLI Diploma and GNVQ level 1; the intermediate level, equivalent to two A levels plus key skills in a technological curriculum; and the advanced level, equivalent to three A levels plus key skills.

Assessment is in the style of NCVQ, by demonstration of practical competence and by the compilation of a portfolio of evidence, combined with externally moderated end of course tests.

The first Tech Bacc courses were piloted in four city technology courses and a consortium of schools and colleges in various TVEI clusters in the Midlands.

International Baccalaureate

These are offered by some schools instead of A levels. Students have to demonstrate achievement at the agreed level of attainment in six subjects selected from a range that straddles the traditional arts/science divide (rather similar to the format for those students taking Scottish Highers and the model proposed by the Higginson Committee in 1988). There is a core programme of general education and subjects are largely assessed by written examination, as for A level. For schools the attraction is the international currency of this award, together with its broader range of subject areas.

It is interesting to note that, within the French system, the *baccalauréat professionnel* (the vocational baccalaureate) or the *baccalauréat technologique* (technical baccalaureate) gives successful candidates the same status of *bacheliers* as those taking the general or technical baccalureates, and gives them the same right of access to higher education. Over 70 per cent of 16–18-year-olds are studying for *baccalauréat* qualifications in France.

Diploma of Achievement

Introduced in 1994 by the Oxford and Cambridge Schools Examination Board, this curriculum enrichment programme is designed to complement A level or GNVQ studies, offering a structured framework for many of the themes previously embraced under the heading of 'general studies'. It aims to meet one of the NTETs by encouraging self-reliance, flexibility and breadth. The course is presented as a cross matrix of *units* (such as getting to know people, the public enquiry project and what is truth?) and *skills* (such as communication, organizing, numeracy, computing, and research and design). The recommended time allocation is four periods a week over four or five terms.

National Vocational Qualifications

NVQs differ from GNVQs in that they relate to assessment of competence in the work place, so that they measure what people can *do* in an occupationally specific area (like animal care, playwork, accounting, retailing or management). Although the focus is work related, some colleges have successfully introduced NVQs for their full-time students by collaborating with local firms and lead industry bodies to establish the particular competencies associated with the different levels, and then securing approval as an accredited body.

The intention of establishing NCVQ in 1986 was to reform the framework of vocational qualifications by creating a system based on high quality standards set by industry. As a result, lead industry bodies (LIBs) were formed to represent interests from within particular occupational areas in the creation of industry specific standards. To date, around 160 of these LIBs have been established. Once standards have been devised, piloted and agreed, awarding bodies such as BTEC, CGLI, RSA and Pitmans, as well as a plethora of professional training organizations, such as the Hotel and Catering

Training Company (HCTC) or the Construction Industry Training Board (CITB), use these standards as the basis for offering qualifications in the specified vocational area.

The qualification is then accredited as an NVQ (and carries the NCVQ logo) and assigned to one of five levels within the national framework of vocational qualifications. These levels range from demonstration of competence in the 'performance of routine work activities' (level 1) through to competence in 'the pursuit of a senior occupation or profession, including the ability to apply a significant range of fundamental principles and techniques' (level 5). The NCVQ framework is intended to embrace the whole age and sophistication range of all vocational occupations, so that, for example, a NVQ level 1 in animal care (accredited by CGLI) would be appropriate for a 16-year-old school leaver who has just been offered a job as an assistant in a cattery or kennel, while NVQ level 4 (accredited by RSA) in training and development would be appropriate for a senior manager in an industrial or commercial organization. Not all occupational areas have qualifications at all of the five levels and most of those developed so far are offered at levels 1, 2 and 3.

Since NVQ standards are all expressed in outcome terms, specified by clear performance criteria, evidence may be provided through accreditation of prior learning and experience, as well as new learning. This means that NVQ programmes do not have to involve the time-serving feature of other post-16 courses. If competence can be demonstrated, then this can be accredited. Each award is built up from separate units of competence, which can be gained separately, so that candidates accumulate credits at their own pace towards the final award.

The NVQ framework is similar to the National Curriculum in the sense that what is to be learnt or demonstrated at each level is clearly specified. However, it differs in that no programmes of study or particular texts are specified for NVQs, so that awarding bodies have considerable flexibility over the design of the programme. Another major difference is that the funding mechanism for institutions offering NVQs (and GNVQs) is partly based on the numbers achieving awards (known as 'output related' funding). Both these differences underpin much of the criticism of 'lack of rigour' that has been levelled at NVQs. Among fashion retailers, for example, there is a difference of opinion about the value of NVQs. While Marks & Spencer and Boots have introduced a programme of training for staff to NVQ levels 1 and 2, others, such as British Home Stores and Burtons, prefer to operate an 'in-house' training scheme, which they regard as more sophisticated.

It is important to note that, of the eight National Training and Education Targets, five are specified in terms of NVQ equivalents (e.g. 60 per cent of young people and 50 per cent of the workforce to reach NVQ level 3 by the year 2000, with 80 per cent having achieved level 2 by 1997). Achievement of these targets is a massive task, which partly accounts for the rapid introduction of the GNVQ in schools and colleges in the early 1990s and the development of 'Modern Apprenticeships' (see page 68). The National Advisory Council for Education and Training Targets (NACETT) reviews progress on the targets, and updates them where necessary.

Youth Training

This TEC funded programme remains the main route by which over 250,000 16- and 17-year-old school leavers who are unemployed can achieve NVQ qualifications. The programme involves an integrated package of 'on' and 'off the job' training, offered through colleges of further education, employers and private training providers.

Following the Dearing Review, the intention is to relaunch the programme as a system of National Traineeships available at foundation, intermediate and advanced levels, providing a vocational progression route to Modern Apprenticeships (see below).

Modern Apprenticeships

Introduced in 1994, this programme was intended to enable more young people to reach NVQ level 3 through employment based training. Employers, TECs and Industry Training Organisations (ITOs) have worked together to develop this initiative, with the reorganized Careers Service playing a key role. Certain occupational sectors (such as agriculture and horticulture, chemical industry, child care, engineering, information technology, marine engineering, retailing, steel industry, travel services) took part in the early pilot schemes, and each designed frameworks that specify the skills, knowledge and understanding which the 'apprentice' is to develop in order to reach NVQ level 3 or above. Units from existing NVQs may be drawn on, and this enables organizations to develop 'multi-skilled' apprenticeships, which require the ability to employ a range of skills across different 'occupational' areas.

Take up was low initially, and the Dearing Review raised the profile of Modern Apprenticeships, stressing the need for early careers advice and guidance in year 9 rather than year 11, so as to provide a better basis for making a more informed choice about this particular post-16 option. The principal target group remains 16- and 17-year-olds and it is hoped that some qualified apprentices will be offered university places on completion of their Modern Apprenticeship.

A major concern for the implementation of the Modern Apprenticeship initiative is that, since it is targeted at the achievement of NVQ level 3, it will turn the Youth Training (National Traineeship) programme itself into the lower tier of a two-track system. Those who are de-selected for the Modern Apprenticeship will be left in a residual Youth Training programme along the lines of the former Mode A and Mode B divisions in the old Youth Training Scheme.

ASSESSMENT AND ACCREDITATION ARRANGEMENTS

With the introduction of GCSEs the jungle of *academic* examinations that existed prior to 1986 was tidied up to some extent. Six regional exam boards oversee the assessment arrangements for GCSEs. 'Quality control' of these exam boards is provided through the monitoring undertaken by the Schools

Curriculum and Assessment Authority (SCAA). For A and AS levels the nine awarding bodies remain as before, and some of these also offer accreditation for Records of Achievement.

The other bodies offering nationally recognized awards (such as ASDAN, BTEC, CGLI and RSA) focus on those courses that are grouped under the broad heading of *vocational*, with NCVQ providing the 'quality control' (it is important to underline that NCVQ is *not*, itself, an awarding body). Many of these courses include an assessed 'key' skills component, for which GNVQs and the ASDAN Award Schemes offer the most developed curriculum framework through which young people can demonstrate these attributes.

Given the proliferation of courses post-16, there has been a clear need for some sort of overarching framework that is understandable by end users (employers and higher education), as well as by students and teachers. The Institute of Public Policy and Research document *A British Baccalaureate* (Finegold *et al.* 1990) presented a framework by which the academic/vocational divisions could be removed. It proposed offering a *single* qualification that subsumed the existing plethora of different qualifications, along the lines of the International Baccalaureate. Subsequent proposals endorsed this view. The White Paper *Choice and Diversity* (DfE 1992) suggested introducing an Advanced Diploma, and the National Commission on Education's report *Learning to Succeed* (1993) recommended an integrated system with a General Education Diploma (Advanced) at 18. Various headteachers' associations and independent schools' networks also stressed their support for this proposal in *Post Compulsory Education and Training*, a joint statement circulated on behalf of AfC, GSA, HMC, SHA, APVIC and SHMIS in October 1994.

The arguments in favour of this were rehearsed and extended, with reference to detailed research and accumulated 'good practice', in *Learning for the Future* (Richardson *et al.* 1995). The issues and implications raised in this excellent report informed the recommendations of the Dearing Review of 1996. There is now widespread acceptance that a genuinely 'unified post-16 curriculum' is the only way to achieve parity of esteem between academic and vocational qualifications, and that this needs to be addressed courageously.

> The direction of reform in other countries suggests that tinkering with our own system and its anachronisms is not enough. We are in a new era, which demands new solutions. More and more countries will achieve high levels of participation and attainment and there will be a blurring of old distinctions between academic and vocational studies, between college and work based learning, and between individual work and teamwork. The challenge is to maximise opportunities for learning in the home, in the workplace, in colleges and in schools, to secure the active participation of individuals in business and the professions, and to harness the power of information technology to give wide access to learning materials. Nationwide networks of learning communities will be the building blocks of 'learning for the future'.
>
> (Richardson *et al.* 1995)

The hope is that 'blurring the distinctions' will mean that access routes to higher education other than through A levels will become the norm rather than the exception; that students will be able to transfer credits from one course to another and move easily between different kinds of qualification (and across the academic/vocational divide); that the needs and aspirations of a much higher proportion of young people in the 14–19 age group will be met and fulfilled.

Currently there are three *main* qualification routes for those in the 14–19 age group:

- GCSEs, AS and A levels (in schools and colleges);
- GNVQs (in schools and colleges);
- NVQs (in employment, with a college or private agency providing training through the Youth Training or Modern Apprenticeship programmes).

The Dearing Review is the most recent in a long line of attempts to reform this structure, so that *each* of these qualification routes will have stated parity of esteem under the framework of *National Awards*, i.e.:

- at the Advanced Level AS and A levels will be equivalent to GNVQ Advanced and the Modern Apprenticeship and other NVQ courses at level 3;
- at the Intermediate Level GCSE grades A to C will be equivalent to GNVQ Intermediate and NVQ courses at level 2;
- at the Foundation Level GCSE D to G will be equivalent to GNVQ Foundation and NVQ courses at level 1.

A levels and GCSEs are intended to develop knowledge, understanding and skills associated with a subject or discipline; applied education courses (e.g. GNVQs) to develop and apply knowledge, understanding and skills relevant to broad areas of employment; vocational training courses (e.g. NVQs) to develop and recognize mastery of a trade or profession at the relevant level. Alongside a re-launch of the National Record of Achievement, all students would also have opportunities to develop and demonstrate their abilities in certain key skills (communication, application of number and information technology), either within the framework of their courses or by pursuing a supplementary course such as the proposed AS level in key skills.

Ron Dearing clearly favoured the retention of the triple track system, and it may be that this was a fudge which does nothing to alter the reality of the lack of parity of esteem. In the drive to establish the enterprise culture in schools and colleges, while protecting the 'gold standard', policy makers may well have overlooked the most critical point in Martin Wiener's (1985) and Corelli Barnett's (1986) analysis, referred to in Chapter 2, of 'cultural disdain' for the practical, particularly within prestigious schools. Tampering with the curriculum focus for the state school system, without addressing that of the private sector, could be considered similar to rearranging the deckchairs on the *Titanic*. An important question to ask about the whole focus of the curriculum reform programme of recent years is 'why is it that the changes (which the government imposed upon the state school system, with so little consultation, preparation or piloting) were imposed on other people's children?' No cabinet minister at that time had a secondary age child at a state school. Is there still an assumption that the leadership (and wealth) of the country will come from private schools and that these children are 'above' or 'outside of' the requirements for the remaining 90 per cent of the population? It could be argued that until *all* schools share a common culture nothing will happen to address the concerns that Wiener and others have articulated, and 'parity of esteem' will simply remain a pious aspiration.

THE CURRICULUM MAP IN TWO SCHOOLS

The intention in this section is to provide examples of what the contemporary curriculum map actually looks like in two different 11–18 schools, and what issues each school has identified in relation to future curriculum development in the light of the various Dearing reviews (1994 and 1996) and other factors. I am grateful to Peter Gallie and Brian Fletcher, headteachers of the respective schools, for the following accounts.

John Taylor High School, Burton upon Trent, Staffordshire

The school is a mixed 11–18 comprehensive school maintained by Staffordshire LEA. There are 1280 students on roll, including 235 in the sixth form. It is situated in Barton-under-Needwood, a large village between Lichfield and Burton upon Trent. The traditional catchment area includes a number of other villages, whose residents commute to Birmingham, Derby and Nottingham. Pupils also come from several small rural villages and a fringe area of Burton upon Trent. The majority of parents probably left school at 16, but are committed to the education of their own children, and there is a significant number of professional parents such as doctors in an area where relatively few children are sent to private schools. The school was founded in 1957 as a secondary modern, and became a comprehensive school in 1971. The buildings date from both these periods.

The curriculum framework

The present curriculum for Key Stages 3 and 4 was phased in five years ago. There are unlikely to be any major changes in Key Stage 3 with regard to National Curriculum requirements. However, the Key Stage 4 curriculum came under review from governors and staff in autumn 1995, with the requirements for all students to take a course in modern languages, technology and religious studies as from September 1996. It was decided that all students should continue with a full modern languages course. The existing core and option requirements (outlined below) were considered educationally valuable and balanced, and give students the opportunity to take a second language, humanity, art or technology subject. If core technology had replaced the creative and practical options block, the arts would have been squeezed into a minimal position; hence the allocation of one period for core technology (which is less than is needed). The two periods of core PE now incorporate health education.

Careful consideration will be given to the possibility of Foundation GNVQ being introduced as a double option at Key Stage 4, although this would break with our philosophy of the past five years that vocationally inclined courses should only be available post-16. There is certainly concern that provision is inadequate for the less academic pupils, but the answer may lie in reviewing the teaching of existing courses, as well as the courses for which students opt.

Post-16 we are giving consideration to the extension of GNVQ courses so as to include manufacturing or travel and tourism, as well as the provision of A level theatre studies.

Key Stage 4

Subject	Periods
English language	4
Mathematics	4
Double science	6
Core technology	1
PE	2
Religious and social education with IT	1
A humanities subject (history, geography, religious studies)	3
A modern language (French, German, Spanish)	3
A practical or creative subject (art, music, drama, food, technology, keyboarding)	3
A choice of art, history, geography, food, German, or keyboarding	3

All core subjects are timetabled in half populations to allow setting; in most subjects this is broad. Option subjects also form ability sets where numbers allow.

All the subjects listed, except core physical education and religious education, lead to GCSE. Core technology leads to a half GCSE so that the majority of students take 9.5 GCSEs.

Post-16

GNVQ Intermediate	Business, health and social care, science. After one year around 40 per cent move to GNVQ advanced courses.
GNVQ Advanced	Business, health and social care. Most students take one A level in addition, or repeat GCSE mathematics or English.
Advanced levels	English literature, mathematics, biology, chemistry, physics, environmental science, history, psychology, geography, religious studies, French, German, art, music, technology, economics.

Current concerns

Our present concerns are far more with helping students of all abilities to improve their capacities and level of performance than with changing the content of the curriculum. There are a number of elements in this:

1 Continuously evaluating the learning activities of pupils within their sub ject areas and the skills or learning approaches they are developing. In this, the new level descriptions given by Dearing provide a little explored guide.
2 Emphasizing the importance of activities in which pupils use knowledge or skills gained in a planned and sustained way, rather than just repro ducing facts or evidence in short answers which demonstrate short-term understanding.
3 Monitoring students' progress: discussing with them points on which they should focus attention for improvement; even setting targets. We are at tempting to build up the role of the class tutor in this respect.
4 Drawing in parents to give every possible support. More frequent reports and discussion with parents on ways young people can be helped.
5 Exploring the use of information technology, both at home and at school, as a learning aid and an aid for orderly and creative expression.
6 Focusing attention on the less academic to help them to a point where they can handle class work autonomously. A whole variety of schemes are being explored, involving one-to-one support from parents, sixth form students and IT.
7 Rewarding improvement. We are currently reviewing all 'reward' systems, aware that students generally appreciate teacher and parent awareness of effort and improvement, but are very self-conscious about public recognition.
8 Stimulating interest. Many of the points above may make learning appear as a soulless and mechanical striving for technical improvement. We are aware that it doesn't work like that. Learning has to be interesting (for most people), and that may depend on group involvement as much as on the subject matter. And variety of activity is important, especially such as field work or visits, where the 'directed' learning may be limited but the contact with the teacher is strong.

Beyond the curriculum framework

We take extra-curricular activities seriously (although I sometimes wonder if we are too 'achievement' orientated). Sport is particularly strong and pop ular, and involves a good number of students at lunch times, during the evenings and at weekends. We aim to offer as wide a range of sports as possible, and this inevitably means drawing in non-PE staff and parents to coach where they have special interest, such as basketball and cross-country running. We are also unashamedly competitive, with teams moving into district, county and national competitions – and winning!

Drama has moved ahead, with a main production – often Shakespeare – each year, and a musical. There is a junior drama club. There are also two concerts and a good variety of musical groups practising at lunch time. In addition to traditional music, there are at least two student bands who rehearse independently and perform periodically. Other activities, such as art and technology, are not run as formal clubs, but have open rooms at lunch times and teachers available – often with lesson time activities spilling beyond lesson time. There is a range of trips, including theatre visits and overseas visits to France and Germany. The sixth form are involved in a number of semi-competitive activities, such as Young Enterprise, Mock Trial and Business Challenge.

I suspect that the comments and descriptions so far show us to be one of a type of 1990s comprehensive school which can be found throughout the country. We are achievement orientated, concerned with improvement and aware of our public image. We are taking most of our students through to a distinctly higher level of qualifications than their parents achieved. We are fortunate in the catchment area and the support we receive, able to establish an ethos and stability which allows most 'problems' to be handled without their becoming crises. I would contend that we present excellent value for money both to parents and to the public (about £1950 per student per year as against the £4500 for private day schools), which isn't often acknowledged.

At the same time there are difficulties. As all organizations find, today's achievements become commonplace tomorrow. Can improvement be sustained? This is particularly significant as funding diminishes, and buildings wear down and look increasingly dated. The strain on staff to mark more, report more and teach more effectively is considerable, and staff grow older. Those students who find achievement difficult can easily become alienated: a dissatisfied minority for whom it is difficult to muster sympathy when we emphasize success, even when we recognize the domestic difficulties which many of them overcome.

There is political pressure for a return to open selection. There are risks that exam qualifications will become the sole objective. I often think that I would like to sit down with other like-minded teachers and work out quite what ideal of comprehensive education we are now aiming towards. Does community still mean anything? Are the values of conventional success exclusive, because some do not share them or cannot achieve them?

Coombeshead College, Newton Abbot, Devon

Coombeshead School was formed in 1975 from an amalgamation of Highweek Secondary Boys and Highweek Secondary Girls schools, when Devon Education Authority abolished 11 plus selection in the area. The annual intake of pupils changed to become comprehensive and was intended to number half of the 11 plus secondary transfer from eight designated primary schools situated in and to the west of Newton Abbot. During the 1980s the annual intake of the school stabilized at around 180, at a time of generally falling secondary school rolls. The school roll in 1985 was 930, with a teaching staff of 50.

The late 1980s witnessed fundamental changes in the government and management of schools. Open enrolment immediately widened the basis of Coombeshead's school intake, so that by 1994 pupils were received from 27 different primary schools, and the annual intake had risen to 230.

In 1989 the school applied to Devon LEA for permission to establish a sixth form and the school was renamed Coombeshead College in 1994 in readiness for its post-16 intake. In the same year the governors were successful in establishing the case for additional accommodation for post-16 students and improved facilities for the entire school population. New science and arts blocks were constructed on the main site. Some 150 students enrolled for post-16 courses in the first year. Nineteen new A level courses were begun, plus a range of GNVQ and NVQ courses to cater for all abilities and most interest. Ten new staff were appointed and the institution seemed to 'grow up' overnight.

The curriculum framework

The Coombeshead curriculum, while largely dictated by the Secretary of State via National Curriculum orders, is quite distinct and reflects the values held by the college and those who work in it. At Key Stage 3 all pupils study English, mathematics, science, history, geography, modern languages, technology, music, art, PE and games, and religious education. At Key Stage 4 the core of mathematics, English, science, modern language, a humanity, an arts subject, PE, RE and three further options permit specialists to enhance their science, languages, humanities or arts subjects.

At Key Stage 4 the college has a long history of offering vocational options, even though the content and the means of accreditation has often changed. The college's general vocational courses coordinator is looking increasingly to plan 14–18 for a continuous and coherent provision, as soon as the means of accreditation can be put in place.

Post-16 the college has had the opportunity to start with a clean sheet. The intention from the beginning was to provide comprehensively for our students. Where we have been unable, through lack of resources, to offer courses to suit all tastes, we have collaborated with other institutions to achieve the students' best interests. Currently we have in place a variety of courses leading to NVQs, which have required close liaison with local companies and with the industrial lead bodies responsible for standards of competence. It has also been our long stated intention to provide education and training for adults, where such provision would enhance the overall provision of our full-time students. Currently 150 adults are enrolled on part-time courses leading to a variety of qualifications. Through such broad post-16 provision we can offer appropriate guidance to students of all abilities, aptitudes and circumstances.

Moving to ten subjects, restricting double scientists to five periods in a 25 period week, restricting core full technology to two periods, restricting double linguists to five, allowing only one core PE period, we have the following Key Stage 4 curriculum:

Core subjects	Periods
English	3
Mathematics	3
Science	3
PE	1
RE	1
Technology	2

Modern language	3
Tutorial	1

Options

History/geography	2
Second Science	2
Arts	2
Vocational	2

Post-16 we have the following curriculum:

GNVQ Intermediate	Leisure and tourism, business, health and social care, art and design
GNVQ Advanced	Leisure and tourism, business, health and social care
NVQs	Motor vehicle, horticulture
Nursery nursing	Certificate course (one year), diploma course (two year)
Advanced levels	Mathematics, English, biology, art, psychology, physics, history, business studies, German, music, drama, community studies, sociology, geography, French, design and technology, chemistry, physical education

Two years ago the government changed the regulations to permit schools to offer further education. The sound engineering course which we franchise from City of Westminster College is an example. Full-time students studying music technology A level join with part-time adults who are keen to achieve qualifications in an area offering growing employment prospects. We plan to offer stage and lighting management via the same route. Similar mixed adult/ full-time student provision is also offered in the areas of child care and nursery nursing, where registered childminders are trained to NVQ standards.

Beyond the curriculum framework

Beyond the National Curriculum throughout Key Stage 3, all students study drama as a discipline in its own right. Through this experience we witness a growth in confidence, in communication skills and presentational skills. Drama is very popular at GCSE, as is our own mode 3 performing arts course, and at A level.

Music provision at Coombeshead is probably the best in Devon. A specialist music course is offered to those capable of joining via audition. We organize and administer an instrumental tuition scheme for about 340 pupils, half of whom attend Coombeshead and half local primary schools. The college has a string orchestra, junior and senior wind bands, various wind ensembles, three choirs, harmony groups and a jazz band. Composition is encouraged and recordings are made in our recording studio, the best equipped in Devon.

Games and PE are encouraged with a generous allocation of time at Key Stage 3 and a very popular optional course at Key Stage 4. Wide ranging facilities permit us to develop teams to compete with other schools at rugby, football, cricket, basketball, athletics, swimming, netball and cross-country.

Residential education has always been highly regarded by the college. In 1987 we refurbished the former primary school at East Prawle for use as a residential centre. All year 7 pupils stay at the centre for a few nights. Specialist art, science, environmental and language weekends take place every year. Until 1996 year 9 pupils also stayed at the centre for a few nights. SATs have taken priority now.

Additional curriculum provision for exceptionally able pupils has been in place for a number of years. Pupils are tested in each of years 7, 8 and 9, and enrichment offered to a group of about 20 in each year in the form of special activities organized by different subject areas and coordinated by a senior member of staff.

The school used to house a unit for 20 pupils with specific learning difficulties. Over many years, therefore, staff expertise was developed in working with 'statemented' pupils. Additional support is given, in class, by a team of five staff qualified and experienced in learning support work.

The pastoral programme is coordinated by heads of year and taught by teams of tutors during weekly sessions. It includes health education and sex education, careers education, environmental awareness, equal opportunities, multicultural awareness, economic awareness, citizenship and behavioural guidance. Every member of the teaching staff belongs to a cross-curricular team or matrix team. In addition, all year 7 non-swimmers are taught to swim; all year 8 pupils study for first-aid qualifications; all years organize charitable activities. Special events are organized every year to promote Europe, women into industry, AIDS awareness and drugs awareness. Prior to our development of a new sixth form, 120 of our leavers went to a local college of FE. Now, fewer than 20 do so. Our sixth form numbers 260 after less than two years in existence. My perception is that more students want to stay on (88 per cent in 1995), but require very positive guidance and tutorial support. They are better placed in a more personal, friendly institution that knows their strengths and weaknesses.

The college was awarded the Schools Curriculum Award for the degree to which it had embraced the resources of the local community to enhance its curriculum. It became Neighbourhood Engineers School of the Year (an award of the Engineering Council and the *Times Educational Supplement*) for its pioneering work in promoting real engineering situations in the science and technology curriculum, which involved close liaison with local firms.

Another significant development has been the introduction of the Youth Award Scheme. Initiated in 1987, it is available for all pupils in years 10 and 11. Recent developments in the scheme have resulted in the incorporation of graduated core skills accreditation for post-16 students, and Coombeshead College is a pioneer in this work. It seems only a matter of time before the accreditation of core skill achievement is a feature of pre-16 work also.

NOTE

1 Research by Sheffield University in 1993 into the performance of 11,000 pupils in Nottinghamshire and Shropshire schools confirmed that the 2.3 per cent increase in A–C grades in 1992 reflected a genuine improvement in standards: see *TES* 23 October 1993.

six

Teachers as curriculum innovators

The case studies of the two establishments in the previous chapter illustrate some of the possibilities for creative responses by schools and colleges to the National Curriculum. And what is clear from any study of the history of curriculum development, as evidenced in Chapter 1, is that teachers *have* been at the forefront of such a process until very recently. The bookshelves of case study literature, evaluation reports and celebration of particular initiatives testify to the profession's tremendous capacity to engage actively in curriculum matters. The Schools Council programmes were just one end of a continuum that saw most schools and teachers actively engaged in curriculum design. The massive expansion of secondary schooling that came with the various baby boom cohorts reaching adolescence, comprehensive reorganization of the 1960s and 1970s, commitments to mixed ability teaching, the raising of the school leaving age in 1972 and the upsurge in work-related activities such as TVEI and School Industry partnerships in the 1970s and 1980s, provided rich opportunities for teachers to take the lead in curriculum development.

The Salters' approach to science teaching, for instance, was a response of a group of teachers and lecturers committed to the notion of 'broad and balanced science for all', and concerned about the failure of science (particularly chemistry) to make links with the lives and interests of young people. Ten years after the pilot development work was undertaken under the aegis of the University of York, more than 500 schools in the UK were involved, with 25,000 students taking nationally set examinations relating to the Salters' courses (Campbell *et al.* 1994).

The Science and Technology in Society (SATIS) project set up by the Association for Science Education (ASE), the professional organization of UK science teachers, aimed to show young people in the 14–16 age group how science and society were interdependent. It arose from the concerns of classroom teachers about the paucity of resources available to support the teaching of GCSEs (Fullick 1992), and it was able to draw on the evaluations of the various initiatives that schools and LEAs had implemented through the Science in Society project of the early 1980s (Kempton and Allsop 1985).

The Advanced Physics Project for Independent Learning (APPIL) was developed by teachers in the ILEA in the late 1970s to encourage students to take a more active role in exploring concepts of physics, seeking out data for themselves and developing independent lines of enquiry (Bodey 1985).

As well as these regional initiatives, national developments, such as the Geography 16–19 Project (Naish and Rawling 1990) and the Microelectronics Education Programme (Thorne 1987), provided rich opportunities, professional support and funding, in some cases, for teachers to translate overarching objectives into school based developments.

It was a time when the professional imagination of teachers was trusted and encouraged to translate educational idealism into classroom practice. This point was reinforced for me in a response to early drafts of this chapter by Peter Gallie, Headteacher of John Taylor High School.

The 1960s and 1970s saw the rapid growth of comprehensive schools with opportunities for rapid promotion as restructuring occurred; the schools also grew with the expansion of teenage numbers. There was a surge of graduates (like you and me), partly impelled by ideals of 'improving society', who found ourselves not in grammar schools, which had attracted graduates previously, but in all ability comprehensives. We found these schools either trying to impose a 'grammar school curriculum for all', or running a secondary modern curriculum alongside the grammar school curriculum in uncomfortable subordination. For the first time, graduates were teaching 'sec mod' children in significant numbers and we found we liked them. There were no suitable text books. So we devised new courses with new resources to suit all abilities. ROSLA reinforced the need for new approaches and the 'new sixth' gave additional opportunities for curriculum development. In many schools there was a core of young staff and we enjoyed the teamwork involved in devising and running new courses.

By the mid 1970s we were already questioning some of the changes we had made. We were aware that, while the 'very able' flourished, the 'quite able' were often insufficiently challenged. There was a need to look at the skills they were developing and it soon became apparent that skills was too simple a word: approaches, competencies, capacities were more appropriate. So there was a shift of emphasis from exciting new content towards resources and teaching approaches designed to develop abilities. At the same time many of us were being promoted and directing our attention to whole school developments, rather than specific curriculum developments. By the 1980s schools were beginning to contract; there were fewer opportunities, less movement, and the influx of graduates diminished. There was also, from within schools, a growing awareness of examination results – partly because better results enabled more to stay into the sixth form, which prevented redundancies as budgetary constraints began to bite. TVEI arrived in the mid 1980s. You mention the flow of curriculum innovation which this introduced. How much of the innovation, made possible by the extra funding, has subsequently faded? Although undoubtedly there were some new ideas and practice generated, I suspect that TVEI was an expensive way of funding limited lasting change.

(Gallie 1996, personal communication)

The TVEI 'story' that Peter Gallie refers to is one that has been well researched by others and referred to already (Gleeson *et al.* 1988; Dale *et al.* 1990, for example). It is clear that, whatever the political motivations may have been behind the introduction of a programme that was funded by the Department of Employment, it provided a ten-year 'window of opportunity' for teachers to take the initiative with regard to curriculum innovation.

Yet in recent years that initiative has been wrested from them. In the run up to the introduction of the 1988 Education Act Kenneth Baker made it clear that 'the system has become producer dominated' (Baker reported in *TES* 1 December 1987). The declared intention was to manage curriculum development from a central agency, effectively marginalizing the influence of professional bodies – and doing so very quickly.

In a case study of an inspirational programme promoting cross-curricular developments as the *basis* for the teaching of academic subjects in four Sheffield secondary schools (along the lines of the primary school 'topic' approach), Alan Skelton charts the rapid change of heart of the teachers involved from energetic expansion in 1987–88 to disillusioned retreat in 1989–90.

The imposition of a subject based National Curriculum framework obviously has enormous consequences for curriculum integration . . . Schools will be legally bound to provide a balanced curriculum for all pupils. Although this is possible within an integrated framework, it will be easier to satisfy external agencies of this fact by following the official 'programmes of study' subject by subject. Most schools will understandably be discouraged from exploring integrated approaches given the extra work load . . . and it is likely that lower status will be afforded such approaches.

(Skelton 1990)

Inevitably, the room for manoeuvre for teachers became increasingly limited, as the workload associated with the implementation of the National Curriculum began to bite. In the years immediately after the 1988 Act teacher led initiatives were put on hold in many schools. Quite apart from dealing with the National Curriculum requirements, local financial management meant that many schools had to invest time in managing contraction and redundancies. The emergence of 'league tables', local authority led 'school reviews' and subsequently Ofsted inspections all created additional bureaucratic requirements with associated pressures. What remained of the concept of professional autonomy was restricted very much to the *how*, not the *what*, of teaching, and the prescriptions of the programmes of study and SATs left precious little creativity for the former. Articles in the *Times Educational Supplement* describing interesting examples of teacher led curriculum development became harder to find, and most of these emerged in LEA areas where TVEI money had arrived later than the rest.

None the less, examples *did* exist, serving as a testimony to the potential still within the profession for curriculum innovation.

Queuing up to conquer male domain
The Creativity in Science and Technology (CREST) award scheme, set up to promote technology in schools, has been flooded with applications from girls. Girls at Weatherhead high school did a survey with the support of Age Concern to identify the problems facing the elderly ... then with the support of the local neighbourhood engineers scheme, they designed and created home-help aids to tackle a range of problems.

(Ian Nash, *TES* 8 January 1991)

Industry pays for a helping of greenstuff
Pupils from six Sheffield schools have designed their own alternative technology education centre and won £250,000 from local and national industry to have it built. The centre will be a model of energy efficiency with solar panels, lighting controlled by the intensity of daylight and energy saving insulation. All materials used to build the centre will be the most environmental friendly available. Sixty 14 year olds drew up six designs and then spent two intensive days consulting the council's architects, engineers and planners. The whole enterprise is the brain-child of David Tuck, Sheffield's design and technology adviser.

(Ian Nash, *TES* 25 January 1991)

Bolton school leads way into new Europe
With 1992 and the single European market looming, the school aims to give next year's leavers a head start by taking all compact graduates on an EC visit next February. During their visits to one of eight towns or cities, including Strasbourg, Paderborn and Berlin, the teams of 10 students, travelling with a youth worker and two teachers, will visit a school, a work place and whatever 'special dimension' a venue may offer.

(Diane Spencer, *TES* 30 August 1991)

Materials gain from juvenile crime wave
Enterprising Durham pupils are studying the criminal mind in a novel attempt to tackle key stage 4 of the national curriculum. The 14–16 year olds are analysing juvenile crime statistics, watching a video on joyriding and visiting the Crown Court as part of a £100,000 project sponsored by Durham Training and Enterprise Council and National Westminster Bank.

(Linda Blackburne, *TES* 20 March 1992)

Under studying
Intake High School is an ordinary looking comprehensive set in an unlovely housing estate, yet a significant number of youngsters from the school have gone on to carve out successful careers in the performing arts ... The course (which was first developed 15 years ago) has been geared to cope with the national curriculum, retaining its integrity,

strength and traditions, yet being fully compliant with what is expected in all core and foundation subjects . . . The philosophy of the school is clearly that children can learn through the performing arts. Staff speak of the spin off for other subjects, success in the performing arts breeding confidence and enthusiasm, so that attitudes to other subject areas are improved. 'We give them a reason for coming to school'.

(Kevin Berry, *TES* 9 October 1992)

Space Odyssey
The space shuttle Endeavour will blast off tomorrow from Cape Canaveral, along with seven astronauts, a Japanese science laboratory – and the first experiment to be sent into space by British schoolchildren. The flight will be the culmination of seven years' work by Ashford School in Kent, whose winning idea was to study the behaviour of chemicals in the weightless conditions of space.

(George Cole, *TES* 11 September 1992)

Age of alchemy
The National Educational Multimedia Awards (NEMA) announced last week, attracted 81 entries and showed that most subject areas and all school sectors are starting to use multimedia software as a standard classroom tool. South Glamorgan certainly got its act together for the awards. The authority submitted 14 separate entries on one CD, which was pressed in house. 'The Heritage Project' from Mount Stuart Primary school, Cardiff, provides a delightful walk around the children's locality, where you click on-screen buildings to enter them and click on-screen people if you want help.

(John Davitt, *TES* 24 August 1994)

Versatile plays
We all know about cross curricular projects, but how many teachers can boast of having used Shakespeare in science (*The Tempest* as a vehicle for studying weather) or PE (a dance version of *King Lear*). A Royal Society of Arts project in association with Leicestershire County Council and the Royal Shakespeare Company has led to 17 primary and secondary schools experimenting with ways of introducing Shakespeare to their pupils.

(Reva Klein, Review section, *TES* 2 April 1993)

Technology? It's a piece of cake
'You can't just miss sugar out because you want to bake a healthier cake. If you're going to alter the recipe, it is vital to experiment and collect the evidence,' says Dawn Grantham, head of design technology at Buckler's Mead school in Somerset, and her sugar free cake lesson is one of several projects which demonstrates seamless links between food studies and the broader technology curriculum.

(Ian Nash, *TES* 26 November 1993)

Out of the pits, into the future
Five years ago Garibaldi School in the Nottinghamshire pit village of Clipstone was losing at least 70 pupils a year to neighbouring schools and was close to the bottom of the county exam league table. Its buildings

were almost derelict and its sports hall had become a haven for drug addicts. The school was on a downward spiral . . . closure was on the cards. But, in an amazing transformation, this apparent no-hope school has been turned into one which has won national and international awards.

(Clare Dean, *TES* 8 April 1994)

Camera ready
Setting up a video camera at the back of the hall and recording the school play is one thing. Making a proper production, working from a film script and going on location is something else, as pupils and staff at De Aston School, a 1000 pupil Lincolnshire comprehensive in Market Rasen discovered when they decided to tackle Jack Rosenthal's play *The Evacuees*.

(Gerald Haigh, *TES* 29 July 1994)

Brockhill Park School
An Environmental Education audit in a Secondary School . . . the first part of the process was to carry out an audit which looked at whether the ethos of the school indicated an interest in and understanding of environmental care; how Environmental Education is managed; where topics, skills and fieldwork appear in the curriculum and for evidence that the school site is used as a learning resource.

(Dawn Munn, *Environmental Education*, Summer 1994, volume 46, p. 10)

The view from South Waikato
'Imagine that instead of a postcard, you're sending a word picture of the view from your window . . . or perhaps you'd rather give your "view" on world affairs or people . . .' That is the suggestion I've been sending over the past year to everyone who has subscribed to 'My View', the Chatback project currently running on the Internet. 'Views' have appeared via electronic mail from all corners of the world – from New Zealand, Hawaii, Estonia, Belgium, Denmark, Hong Kong, South Africa, Canada, the US and Britain.

(Pat Davidson, *TES* 11 August 1995)

Heads together
The inhabitants of Portland Island are getting used to coming across geography students armed with clipboards and a list of questions about what it's like to live at the southernmost tip of Dorset. If an enterprising partnership between the county's planning and education departments achieves its aims, it's likely there will be more visitors on the trail. Planners and geographers have a lot in common and when they work together both sides can benefit.

(Mary Cruickshank, *TES* 2 February 1996)

On a roll to the right framework?
Integrated learning programmes, and significant elements of modularisation in years 9 or 11 have more than a ring about them of the 1970s

trendiness that HM Senior Chief Inspector has recently condemned. Yet last year's Ofsted inspection rated Sandringham 'very successful'. The school offers a teaching programme that goes well beyond the national curriculum. It provides a quality of education which is 'different, challenging, and sometimes extraordinary'. The innovative modular programme enables pupils to follow a core programme of national curriculum subjects, with opportunities to take a number of options on a term by term basis. Staff have to re-write large chunks of schemes of work and assessment to fit the one term framework. The trick is to make up the modules from the coursework component of the subject.

(Michael Duffy, *TES* 22 March 1996)

These, and many other examples in the pages of the educational press, demonstrate that teachers are still very active on the curriculum front, notwithstanding all the contemporary pressures they face. Innovation and inspiration are still much in evidence, despite the increase in 'paperwork' that most teachers decry. But why hasn't the profession simply acquiesced to the constraints of the National Curriculum and its associated assessment framework? Why haven't teachers just focused down on 'delivering' their respective subjects in accordance with National Curriculum requirements? Why do so many give themselves what seems like extra work?

Writing in the spring 1993 edition of *Forum*, Roger Seckington offered one answer.

There are sound reasons why the creative energies of teachers are focused on ensuring the best outcomes . . . the overriding concern remains with the students at Key Stage 4 who must be given the best possible deal by teachers, and that means working effectively in the real world . . . The national curriculum will be made to work because hard working teachers will do their best to create some order from the current chaos, so that the young people in their care are not disadvantaged. It is a great pity that more is not left to the professionalism of teachers.

(Seckington 1993)

In *Learning to Succeed*, published in 1993, the National Commission on Education also drew attention to the creative force for change within the teaching profession, urging that decision makers at all levels of education take note of innovative practice.

Innovation involves discovering new ideas, developing methods of applying those ideas to particular problems or situations, and bringing them into use on a wide scale. In Britain we have always rated highly the ability to discover new ideas. We have attached less importance to their development, and all too often we have been poor at implementing them generally.

The report highlighted a number of examples of innovative practice, which complement those culled from the pages of the *Times Educational Supplement* that are listed above.

- The Cognitive Acceleration through Science Education (CASE) Project, which used new approaches to teaching science to develop higher level thinking in pupils aged 11–13. Research showed that participating pupils subsequently performed significantly better in science, English and mathematics GCSEs than did a control group, more than doubling the number of passes at grade C or above.
- Flexible learning, an approach encouraged by TVEI, encourages students to take more responsibility for their own pace of study. A study of a flexible learning project concerned with the teaching of geography to GCSE groups demonstrated a higher level of achievement among pupils using flexible learning compared to others taught in more traditional ways. Equally significant was the observation that 'pupils of all ages and abilities reported an increase in motivation and that they worked harder and for longer on more effective learning activities.'
- The use of information technology to enrich the quality of learning. 'At Wirral Metropolitan College, for example, the use of IT has increased study time by an average of five hours a week per student, without increasing staff resources. It is also making college facilities available to employers and others in the community.

The Commission recommended the establishment of a Council for Innovation in Teaching and Learning, with a brief that included the evaluation of new teaching and learning methods and materials, and the effective dissemination of such research to education and training providers and professional organizations.

In the same report though, the Commission noted the low morale amongst the teaching profession:

> The introduction of the national curriculum, the new framework for assessment on teacher morale and the frequent changes to both, often at very short notice, have created a huge increase in teacher workload, especially through administration and paperwork. Few teachers enjoy this; it is not what they entered the profession for. The effects are shown in the increase in the number of resignations due to ill health which have nearly trebled since 1979 ... and a disturbing incidence of job related stress amongst teachers.

At the time of the publication of the National Commission's report, the NUT commissioned a research project to identify teachers' views on aspects of the 14–19 curriculum. Led by Professor Sally Tomlinson of Goldsmiths' College, the research team interviewed a range of teachers in a geographically representative group of schools.

Among its conclusions the project team reported that:

> Teachers resent the imposition of a curriculum into which they feel they had minimal input, even the Dearing slim down. They support the development of a curriculum, in partnership with central and local government, governors, parents, employers, with some input from the local community and pupils.

> (NUT 1995a)

As an indicator of the mood of the profession this study revealed some important concerns.

> Ideally they would like a broad, flexible curriculum for all students, which encompassed a range of subjects and experiences; a breadth of knowledge and skills; the development of critical faculties; opportunities and choice for all; scope for individual learning; no early specialisation; no arts–science divide; no academic–vocational divide. There was considerable support for a modular, flexible curriculum with core courses for all students.
>
> (Tomlinson 1995)

The report demonstrated remarkable unanimity among the professionals on nearly every issue, including opposition to selection for separate schools at 11 or 14, and the GCSE in its present form. Increasingly, it seems, teachers recognize the significance of the 14–19 progression: the fact that most pupils continue post-16 renders a 'final' exam at 16 less necessary, and argues for a post-16 course along the lines of the International Baccalaureate.

Teachers may have been marginalized by the 1988 Act and subsequent legislation in terms of influencing the shape and structure of curriculum development, but the *capacity* for innovation is clearly as present as it was in the 1960s and 1970s. As concern rises over some of the negative consequences of recent legislation, there are signs of a reassertion of the professional spirit and a rekindled willingness in some quarters to harness this energy. Tim Brighouse, who has done so much to inspire a reconstruction of educational provision in the city of Birmingham, outlined his thinking in the *TES* 'Greenwich Lecture' of 1994.

> It seems to me there are three basic elements to teaching which are parts of what I call the 'golden cracker'. The first involves getting to know the child, the second involves the child practising skills, doing exercises, being occupied in consolidation of learning and the third is what I have called the alchemist's stone – the teacher's skill in intervening to stretch the pupil's learning . . . To mark the learner's mind we need to know its intricacies, its preferred learning styles, its different sorts of intelligence – motor, linguistic, spatial, musical, logical, scientific, personal. We need to know that the pupil's mind stands ready to do a deal with the other end – the teacher's extraordinary skill as an alchemist to the mind in transforming mental slavery to freedom. At this end lies the golden cusp of the teacher's skill: his or her ability to open the mind.
>
> (Brighouse 1994)

Tim Brighouse went on to offer a case study of one of Birmingham's 'many excellent schools', a school in which the teachers were engaged in 'intensive, subtle, sensitive, but insistent questioning' at the 'frontiers of learning'. Undaunted by the task confronting him on his appointment as chief education officer to an authority that had been severely criticized by the government for its poor standards, Tim Brighouse set out to transform the levels of achievement in Birmingham schools. The man who had successfully challenged John Patten's libellous description of him as a 'nutter' gave himself a number of targets, including one of visiting every school in the authority during his first year of office. His capacity to enthuse and inspire is legendary, as is his ability to transform problems into opportunities (Brighouse 1996). He demonstrates the power of vision and stamina.

We are going to capitalise on our teachers and the hopes of all our parents for the next generation. Together we are applying the lessons of research and we are backed by formidable political will. The pride of the city, which was the cradle of local government, does not admit any outcome other than a certainty that we shall succeed.

(Brighouse 1994)

Although Tim Brighouse is remarkable for his capacities to put fire into the heart of practitioners, he is not alone in his belief that teachers should assert their very real skills as professionals. The issue of the *Times Educational Supplement* that carried the responses of teachers to Chris Woodhead's annual report (illustrated at the end of Chapter 2) also reported a talk by Professor David Bridges of the University of East Anglia on the occasion of the *Cambridge Journal of Education*'s twenty-fifth anniversary lecture. It referred to his 'rallying call to revive the intellectual excitement and innovative spirit of the 1960s and 1970s . . . We have to oppose and subvert the enervating control and censorship which Government agencies are exercising over the curriculum for schools . . .' (Hofkins 1996b).

As celebrations for the twenty-first century hot up, debates about the purpose of education will resurface, alongside discussions about underpinning values and beliefs. The curriculum ground will be fiercely contested again, as scarcity of resources and limited employment opportunities raise further challenges to traditional responses. Politicians of all shades will be forced to re-examine cherished ideologies.

In an article in *The Guardian* in March 1996, Bob Moon urged David Blunkett, the then Shadow Education Minister, to drop the outdated ideas contained in a speech he had made the previous week about education renewal.

Within New Labour there is an articulate group which seems determined to foist the now fading rhetoric of the outdated new right on to an education policy for the next millennium. Will Hutton's otherwise brilliant analysis of *The State We Are In* and Mandelson and Liddle's polemic, published this week, are two examples of a vision of education straight out of the 1950s. Harriet Harman's school choice would be a third. They have little time for comprehensive schools, recognise few achievements, and have swallowed the anti-teacher polemic hook, line and sinker. Blunkett seems to have one foot in all that . . . and his analysis misses out a number of important dimensions. How, for example, can a still overtly prescriptive and conformist national curriculum be made to achieve the diversity Labour seeks? And what of teachers? Have any professionals other than politicians received such a drubbing over the past few years. In *Excellence for Everyone* Labour offered a New Deal for teachers. It is vitally important that this is at the core of policy.

(Moon 1996)

There are signs that the curriculum pendulum is beginning to swing back again. There is more consensus among teachers than there has been for many years about the importance of certain goals and a reassertion of professional control of the form and content of many aspects of schooling.

Modular A levels, which the government proscribed at the beginning of the decade, are now back in fashion. A glance down the SCAA lists of qualifications approved by the Secretary of State (DfE 1995) reveals that school based development is still active. Many exam boards are accrediting school (or LEA) specific GCSEs. Despite the criticisms (Smithers 1993, for example), GNVQs have succeeded in sustaining enthusiasm for further education among a huge cohort of 16–19-year-olds who would previously have abandoned the system. There is a recognition that LEAs still have a role to play in relation to curriculum development.

> Curriculum development, as a function of LEA, is almost dead. Almost. There is a degree of optimism in the word. I sense a wakening desire to revive it, a realisation that someone needs to get teachers together across schools, to give time to developing their best ideas.
>
> (Sofer 1995)

Teachers themselves, as revealed by the responses in Chapter 7, are generally more involved than they have ever been in curriculum development, and more aware of the social and political context in which they are working. The government 'reforms' of the past ten years have served to 'politicize' teachers in a way that union membership had not managed to do in the whole of the previous century. In the spring of 1995 Roehampton Institute ran a conference entitled 'Re-thinking UK Education: What Next?' The abstracts of the principal contributors were published in the *Times Educational Supplement* under the heading 'Teachers – the forgotten heroes' (Hargreaves *et al.* 1995). A common argument was that teachers needed to be in the vanguard of educational reform and curriculum innovation.

There is an unparalleled opportunity to harness the expertise and the commitment that still exists. Educational policy makers who put their faith in a reassertion of professional autonomy may be richly rewarded.

As is so often the case with the *Times Educational Supplement*, the last word comes from Ted Wragg.

> If there is a change in Government, then the one thing the whole nation needs is a dramatic change in tone and style. The macho assumption that willy-nilly, state 'toughness' is always best, whether with teachers, children or society at large is manifestly garbage. Acting tough should be saved for when it counts, not be the first line of defence.
>
> I blame Margaret Thatcher, who deluded herself that she got Government off our backs when the opposite was the case. Her deep distrust of her own colleagues, and of professional groups like teachers and doctors, led to a climate of deep suspicion instead of partnership, so what followed was inevitable.
>
> The first national consequence was a macho style of management in which professional people had to be told, by prats like Kenneth Clarke,

exactly what and what not to do. Hence the endless bureaucracy and form filling, as teachers, doctors and other groups, in the absence of trust, are compelled to write everything down for inspection.

The second inescapable result was a proliferation of crackpot unworkable policies. Since the professions are scorned, advice is sought outside them, so any barmy think-tank or pressure group, instead of being shown to the nearest padded cell, is given greater credibility than teachers and doctors. The latter are seen as 'vested' or 'producer' interest, while the former, however daft, are said to be the true voice of the consumer.

The third and most unpleasant outcome has been a general climate of stomach churning conflict, instead of harmony and partnership. This must change as the 21st century dawns ... Don't set teachers against families when both are supposed to be on the same side. Try asking one or two practitioners for a bit of informed advice. It wouldn't come amiss after all these years.

(Wragg 1996)

seven

The profession's perspectives

What do teachers make of all this?

Earlier chapters have examined the historical context of curriculum development and the way in which some aspects of professional autonomy have been reduced by events and policies. However, in outlining the curriculum map for the 14–19 age group, Chapter 6 illustrated ways in which the profession has continued to exercise some initiative with regard to curriculum matters. Is this a reflection of the profession's resilience to external interference, or have teachers generally accepted the ascendancy of government control?

The National Commission on Education report *Learning to Succeed* (1993) referred to 'low morale', and there is plenty of talk about 'escape committees' in school staffrooms.

In his second annual lecture in 1996 the Chief Inspector for Schools accused teacher unions, chief education officers, academics and education journalists of inciting neurosis in the profession. 'It is dangerous in the extreme to play to the lowest common denominator of professional anxiety.' Was he right to be so dismissive of 'professional anxiety'? Perhaps, a more important question is 'was he wise?'

What do teachers themselves think of what's been happening? The research undertaken by Sally Tomlinson and the NUT team in 1995, referred to in Chapter 6, highlighted considerable underlying concern among teachers. The feeling that their professional view has been marginalized is universal, and there is alarm about the consequences.

In its eagerness to apply the ideology of the market place to the state sector of schooling, the government has done its best to exclude the profession from serious debate about curriculum issues. As was indicated in Chapter 4, by comparison with the way other countries have approached curriculum change, this is unusual. The example of Spain, where consultation with all interest groups took three years *after* initial proposals were published, is more the norm than the exception (Weston and Stradling 1993). It would seem

that the Conservative government deliberately chose to ignore the accumulated wisdom of history, and that we are now reaping the consequences.
Although draft proposals were circulated for 'consultation' by the DES, the
general feeling among the profession was that this exercise was simply 'window dressing'. Julian Haviland's research into the responses received by the
DES prior to the 1988 Act gave a lot of credence to this point of view
(Haviland 1988).

There are some who see the whole exercise of the 1988 Education Act and
its aftermath as a cynical and manipulative move to re-establish the grammar school system, and reinforce the privilege of the independent sector.
The ideology of the market place has driven more and more schools (and
parents) to opt for a curriculum focus that enhances their position in the
league tables. The value system is one that promotes competitiveness as
opposed to cooperation, and would entirely explain the exclusion of a profession which might have another set of values to overlay on this view
(Woods 1995).

So what does this body, with its strong sense of values, think about what
has happened?

In the spring of 1996 a questionnaire was circulated to teachers and lecturers in every school and college involved in the ASDAN Award Scheme.
The purpose of the questionnaire was clearly explained: to elicit and represent views of teachers about how things are in schools today and how they
might have changed over the past twenty years. It was designed to ascertain
four things:

1 The experience and extent of teacher and lecturer involvement in curriculum innovation.
2 Views about how this involvement had changed over their time in
  teaching.
3 Views about their current status and how this may (or may not) have
  changed over the years.
4 Views about the significance of the ASDAN Award Scheme.

Almost by definition the group surveyed represent the innovative end of
the profession – since they had voluntarily chosen to take part in the ASDAN
Award Scheme at a time when every establishment in the country was suffering from 'initiative overload'. To take the Award Scheme programme forward in their respective establishments will have required careful negotiation
with senior management and governing bodies, skilful presentations to parents and pupils, and a large amount of time beyond the contracted 1265
hours to design and implement the curricular model. The Award Scheme
network of registered establishments offered both an obvious template for
undertaking such a survey and a mechanism for tapping into the thinking of
a group of people who had clearly demonstrated their professional potential.

One hundred and ninety questionnaires came back, slightly higher than
the 10 per cent return that is the usual response for a postal survey. Given
that the questionnaire demanded more than just a tick box response, this is
impressive. All the questions were open ended, inviting detailed response.
And from these responses it has been possible to paint some kind of picture

of professional concerns. The sample was extensive enough throughout the UK and across a range of establishments (independent schools, comprehensive schools, colleges of further education, sixth form colleges, special schools and off-site units) to be considered 'representative', although it is likely (for the reasons given already) that it is representative of the committed end of the profession – far removed from the 'ineffective' and 'failing' end of the spectrum lambasted by Ofsted.

I am particularly grateful to all those who responded. Their names are listed in the appendix (except in the very few instances where anonymity was requested). It must have taken a lot of time and thought to pen the replies, and I feel that the willingness to take such trouble to register concerns, suggestions and observations speaks volumes itself about the capacity of the profession to make a measured and valued contribution to any debate about curriculum development. I trust that the collective voice will be heard by those responsible for constructing the educational policy that will shape the system for the twenty-first century.

The responses are grouped under headings that directly relate to the original questions. Within each heading I have attempted to cluster comments around a particular focus, so as to paint as broad and coherent a canvas as possible from the replies received. Responses to the specific question about the ASDAN Award Scheme are given at the end of Chapter 8.

TEACHER AND LECTURER INVOLVEMENT IN CURRICULUM INNOVATION

Question 1: Since you started teaching, what kinds of curriculum development work have you been involved with in your establishments?

What was most significant about the responses here was the remarkable range of activities described. As a yardstick of professional commitment, the list itself stands as a testimony to the tremendous capacity of teachers and lecturers to engage in innovative work.

Teachers reminisced fondly about their previous involvement with CSE Mode 3 and some of the Schools Council programmes referred to in Chapter 2, such as the Humanities Curriculum Project (HCP) and Geography for the Young School Leaver (GYSL), or the Nuffield Science Project. One or two could even recall ROSLA schemes! The various forerunners of the National Record of Achievement (NRA) were noted by many of the older teachers: the Record of Personal Experience (RPE), the Record of Personal Achievement (RPA), the Oxford Certificate for Educational Achievement (OCEA), 'lifeskills' courses and the NPRA.

The pre-vocational programmes that emerged in the early 1980s, such as City and Guilds 365, Design for Living, the BTEC/CGLI Foundation Programmes and the Certificate of Pre-vocational Education (CPVE), were all listed, as were programmes concerned with raising the achievement of certain groups, such as the Lower Attaining Pupils Programme (LAPP) and the Certificate of Extended Education (CEE). Almost all the questionnaire returns described active involvement in work related curriculum activities: TVEI/ TVEE, Compact schemes, Mini Enterprise, Young Enterprise, Project Trident, Understanding Industry and the ubiquitous work experience and careers guidance programmes, which often operate alongside college link courses.

Reflecting on years past, in some cases as far back as the early 1960s, it was clear that curriculum innovation had been a way of life for many staff. After listing two columns of acronyms, one teacher wrote 'God, I must lie down for a while!' Just noting the extensive range of activities that the profession had initiated was time consuming enough: the implementation of these activities was another experience and one which many teachers and lecturers were clearly very willing to explore. What shone through the sheets of questionnaire returns about what people had been doing was professional commitment.

And this commitment burns no less brightly today than it did twenty years ago. The acronyms may have changed, alongside the source of funding; but teachers and lecturers are still in there devising and designing new courses and programmes. Music workshops, theatre productions, arts programmes, school orchestras, video production units, information technology clubs, school newspaper and magazine editorial teams, dance groups, eisteddfods and electronics clubs all affirm that teachers' commitment to the aesthetic and creative is alive and well. These opportunities for young people sit alongside a plethora of sporting events, outdoor pursuits and recreational activities on offer in schools, such as inter-school fixtures, residential field trips, landscape gardening, traffic education, riding for the disabled, Trail Blazer schemes, driving awareness, the Ten Tors expedition, skiing and a whole range of lunch time and after-school clubs catering for interests as diverse as chess, structural phonics, Latin and astronomy.

At the same time national programmes such as the Duke of Edinburgh's (D of E) Award scheme, Amateur Swimming Association (ASA) Awards, St John Ambulance Three Cross Award, St Ivel Award Scheme, Sports Leader Awards and the CREST Awards continue to attract support from schools and colleges, with comparative newcomers like the ASDAN Award Scheme, the Diploma of Achievement and the Liverpool Enrichment programme providing a much needed mechanism for accrediting a broader profile of achievement – the former doing so successfully across the whole 14–19 ability range.

Quite apart from the inevitable references to GCSEs, Key Stage 4 curriculum developments and GNVQs, teachers and lecturers made a point of highlighting the current menu of pre-vocational programmes (such as the CGLI Diploma of Vocational Education, the RSA Initial Awards, Wordpower and Numberpower), and the various activities that are embraced by the broad heading of personal and social education (PSE). Community service, international exchange programmes, school councils and 'core skills' programmes are also very much in evidence, as are focused courses designed to 'stretch' the high fliers, such as an 'able learners' course and Somerset Thinking Skills.

It is an impressive canvas of activity and bears witness to the sort of values and commitment that Tim Brighouse was celebrating in his reference to the 'golden cusp of the teacher's skill' (page 86). Teachers and lecturers in schools and colleges throughout the UK are demonstrating not only their professional imagination but what this imagination can actually achieve. Their clear ability to continue to transform the experience of their students, despite all the concerns about underfunding, poor resources, inadequate buildings and fears of redundancies, gives teachers and lecturers the moral right to have their opinions listened to in any debate about curriculum matters.

The hope is that the comments and concerns expressed in the sections that follow will provide some food for thought and action. Theirs is a voice that policy makers can't afford to ignore.

CHANGING INVOLVEMENT OVER THE YEARS

Question 2: Could you offer any comments on how your involvement in curriculum development has changed over the years?

'Promotional opportunities enable you to have a more direct influence'

My role has changed from being solely involved at the delivery point to being a coordinator of curriculum initiatives, responsible not only for delivery but for INSET, accessing funding, chairing teams of teachers with a given brief – such as selecting qualifications for vocational education.

(P. Collins)

My promotions have given me greater responsibility in managing the curriculum. However, the many changes have not allowed for proper development – just responding to the next change/imposition. I cite the recent KS4 review as a case in point.

(G. Wild)

Promotional opportunities enable you to have a more direct influence on the implementation of the initiatives suggested. It would have been difficult to launch ASDAN without the influence and backing of the senior management group. Being part of senior management and promoting initiatives has implications for being involved and making projects work successfully.

(Mike Creary)

I am now more likely to get involved in curriculum development than before. I have more of a managerial post, therefore more non-contact time to think about what I do. Positive experiences of involvement with the Youth Award Scheme means I am more confident about approaching peers and senior management team with ideas and 'know how', so as to access money more efficiently.

(Kath Grant)

My involvement has developed since my appointment as Head of Sixth Form and concomitant responsibilities for overseeing complementary studies programme. So far developments have been prompted by our students' needs – this might be subsumed by legislation.

(Anne Clifford)

For me it has changed from being on the fringe with GCSE, to instigating and offering the Youth Award Scheme to all students in Years 10 and 11. I am now much less the recipient of doing a course myself than developing and putting courses in front of the Senior Management Team (SMT) and the governors.

(Derek Hadden)

As a senior teacher, I am responsible for forward planning with senior management colleagues. Much of our work has been in best-guessing, especially in the light of Dearing's proposals.

(Mike Carver)

I progressed from being a young, naive curricular assistant in the eighties to a head of department with progressive ideas. This took a massive kick in the early nineties with the National Curriculum. Now, as a deputy principal, I try to stimulate teachers into developing curriculum initiatives within the framework of National Curriculum and GCSEs – which I still believe is possible and becoming more so.

(Eric Winstone)

Through promotion I have more say in content, methodologies, and such like. Also I have gained an MEd which has offered me opportunities to see what is happening elsewhere – meeting colleagues, and so on.

(Anon)

On starting teaching I had little or no say over school policy although I could teach what I felt children needed. Now I am on the senior management team and a school governor, and so have a lot of input on school policy; but, due to National Curriculum, my hands are tied to a great extent regarding what I want to teach. In my field of special education I feel we have lost a lot of good therapeutic work due to pressures of the National Curriculum and threat of Ofsted.

(Colin Whittaker)

'There is now much less scope for teacher initiative'

I believe that we have had too much professional judgement taken away from us. Although the National Curriculum has had some great benefits for subject areas, I still struggle with its assessment and inflexibility. Having worked for 15 years in the system, I'm aware that some of the excellent practice experienced in the early eighties has been lost and forgotten.

(Karen Jenkins)

There is now much less scope for teacher initiative. PSE and GCSE coursework modules are perhaps the only areas remaining. Moreover, the lack of consultation with teachers over the details of the National Curriculum reflects government indifference (or hostility?) towards teachers' views.

(Dr Richard Gurnham)

I started teaching in the last year of CSE/O level and my involvement in curriculum development has not changed at all. It has been a constant process of initiating schemes and programmes only to see further change before any refinement of the process could occur. It amazes me that we, as a profession, still find time and energy for enrichment on top of all of this.

(Clive Baker)

There have been many changes in the last 5–6 years, especially in syllabus content and assessment procedures at GCSE and A level. These changes are the result of government/SCAA led initiatives rather than 'teacher-led'.

(Judy Miles)

In the past, courses were teacher-led and teacher-marked. Now with the National Curriculum all courses are prescriptive, with very little room for development and very little time to explore interesting facets.

(Paul Fursland)

The developments I have increasingly become involved in have been more about setting up structures and record keeping than with teaching and learning styles – although that is where my heart is! There is more emphasis on student independence, with skill learning and action planning playing an increasing role.

(Hazel Saunders)

Curriculum development seems to be a perpetual aspect of teaching now – not just development of ideas and fine tuning of systems, but massive total reinventions. Life is one long new initiative!

(J. Jones)

There is less room and time available – and less scope, as most activities must contribute to league tables.

(Graham Wright)

When I started teaching there was a general expectation that most of the staff would be involved in some kind of enrichment on a 'good will' basis. When the set number of hours to be worked came in (1987?) much of that type of activity faded out. It appears to be returning to some extent, but there is a horrible emphasis on finance.

(Christie Drakeley)

The emphasis has moved from actually inventing a course from nothing to organizing an already 'made-up' course. My schemes of work are now not mine but a GCSE board or National Curriculum one. Even lessons plans are not my own!

(Jacalin Chawner)

The National Curriculum has put a great strain on those in special education (especially in the Moderate Learning Difficulty (MLD) arena). Ofsted expects MLD pupils to follow the National Curriculum and sit GCSEs. It is difficult to disapply pupils from whole parts of the National

Curriculum and it is logistically impossible to timetable to allow for some parts of the National Curriculum to be disapplied. The National Curriculum has narrowed the children's experience rather than bene-fited it. All our extra-curricular activities are done through staff's good will, voluntarily in their own time.

(Kiri Garbut)

Recently, because of funding criteria, we have had to be more 'exam' directed. Initially we were looking at the benefits to the students and, although this still applies, I wonder if we would have had to fight for our core skill provision if we were not given directives from outside bodies.

(Pete Sinfield)

It has become much more focused on accredited schemes and core skills recently.

(Jane Williams)

It has been too constraining. 'Thou shalt deliver the core skills' being the eleventh commandment. What is important is that pupils receive an education that they feel happy with and is useful for their purposes. I admit that maths, English, science and humanities are important but they can be delivered via other vehicles.

(John Goldring)

When we started work on the humanities scheme we had a level playing field, in that very few outside constraints were placed upon us. We led INSET training and consulted other staff, and the results really reflected our philosophy and our attempt to offer the students a relevant and enriched learning. Currently we are writing curriculum statements ever mindful of Ofsted, and the National Curriculum. Whereas before we were led by the belief that we were providing knowledge, experiences and chances to develop attitudes and skills, we are now led by the wooden dictates of the system.

(Frank Byle)

'It's gone full circle'

In my early teaching career I had some involvement with Mode 3, which developed with experience. There has always been room for pro-active staff to become involved in new initiatives – but it is very depend-ent upon time available. The changes in the National Curriculum have put pressure on all staff and fewer are volunteering to become more actively involved. Access to funding via careers or TECs can help to give time to develop initiatives.

(E. Evans)

With the proposed introduction of GNVQs and NVQs and the future involvement of schools, we appear to have come full circle. The need to measure progress and outcomes in a sensible way will eventually be mastered, but we appear to be moving in the right direction. GNVQs allow a greater degree of input and innovation from teachers, but within an assessment framework. This can only be beneficial in reintroducing teachers back into the mould of taking charge of day to day education, and away from the rigid targets that emerged in the initial outline of the National Curriculum.

(Mike Creary)

'Variety within order' should be the motto for all curriculum development: a clearly defined structure supporting teacher led initiatives based on knowledge and understanding of the varying needs of varying students. There is a need for a coherent framework to avoid reinventing the wheel, but within that structure, teachers can be autonomous professionals working to develop the potential of all students.

(Anne Clifford)

From the Record of Personal Achievement (RPA) to ASDAN I have seen a completely full circle. I have been involved in separatist and mixed ability thrusts, in supporting within the classroom, and withdrawing students from it. I've watched us go from learning centred to child centred to learning centred.

(Anon.)

Being an optimist, I think that once the profession has a chance to fully appreciate the flexibility that Dearing has re-introduced, there will be considerable scope for creativity. But at present it is difficult to appreciate enhanced freedom at a time when new syllabuses must be in place for September. We need breathing space in order to make considered responses, which are in the best interests of our students.

(Pam Taylor)

My personal involvement has changed from a talk, chalk and shut up attitude towards one of giving pupils more responsibility for their own learning. In older students this nurtures self discipline, pride in work and increased motivation.

(Mo Pepper)

It has gone from a child-centred with no real shape, to a more focused child-centred, then a sharp move to a content led discrete subject based formula, which has softened a bit in the last two years to allow more scope for developing extra curricular themes.

(Austin Howard)

I feel that education is slowly drifting back to where it was in the hands of a good teacher prior to the innovations. Witness the rewrites of the National Curriculum compared to what we were doing prior to the mess! Much could be written about what has been lost from education in the changes (like inter-school collaboration) but much could also be written about what teachers as professionals and guardians of quality have been able to retain (like the ASDAN Award Scheme) through sheer professional commitment. League tables direct this commitment into a narrow and impoverished provision.

(Graham Wright)

It has virtually gone full circle in the last ten years. It started with CSE Mode 3 (English), then GCSE 100 per cent coursework, then National Curriculum requirements including SATs and GCSE exam preparation. Now the pendulum is swinging the other way, giving up on National Curriculum for Special Educational Needs (SEN) pupils – giving them the essentials of what they need to know, planning courses based on Youth Award Scheme or RSA, because we would be doing them a disservice if we taught them French or history but not how to get on a bus or budget carefully.

(Mike Bullen)

'TVEI changed curriculum development dramatically'

When I first started, I taught on Mode 3 CSE courses and that was good. I then spent some years in the independent sector (special schools) and had to invent lots of things, but alas, of only temporary duration. TVEI was the next initiative and it was good as well, but unfortunately short-lived. The work I did for TVEI fed into the early work I started with the Youth Award Scheme at this school, and I have attempted to keep the same ethic of student independence going in the Youth Award Scheme, as well as my departmental work.

(Steve Heigham)

TVEI changed curriculum development dramatically, as it offered a framework and a structure in which developments could be planned and evaluated.

(Martin Wilcox)

I had no direct involvement until TVEI came along, when I became part of the process of flexible learning, helping to organise media days, and industry days. It was at that time that the Diploma of Vocational Education was introduced in years 10, 11 and 12, and I became part of the curriculum development team looking at vocational education, careers, work experience and so on. Over the last two years I have also helped a local high school introduce GNVQ and the Youth Award Scheme.

(Philippa Wadsworth)

I was involved in new curriculum developments while lecturing in colleges of FE. I moved to an adviser's post to take forward curriculum initiatives through TVEI funding.

(Veronica Lawrence)

In 1989 I was appointed as a TVEI development officer, which included extensive training in managing change and curriculum development. In 1992 the curriculum development was extended from 14–16 to include the whole school (5–16 years). I also became a member of the senior management team, a position which will terminate at the end of TVEI. In 1994 I became responsible for accreditation, and therefore coordinate Youth Awards.

(Elaine Poppleton)

'Curriculum development must reflect students' needs'

I think developments like the Youth Award Scheme and student and staff responses to it run in the face of the utilitarian and mechanistic curriculum forced upon us. The pressure to 'produce' labour for a failing post industrial economy and the mechanisation and de-skilling of teaching go hand in hand. Things like YAS and other equally valid enrichment examples give me the hope that education can still be seen from a broader viewpoint than purely assessment driven criteria.

(Clive Baker)

The high points in my career have been involvements in developing 'Geography in the changing world' and the ASDAN Award Scheme. Pupils love the sense of achievement offered by these programmes.

(Colin Twigg)

Probably the best single most rewarding and effective change to have taken place in my particular school in recent years has been the complete creation of new curriculum framework which takes account of our ethos, aims and objectives over three Key Stages. What has been interesting has been the teacher led move to evaluate and review the new system and develop it in a consistent and on-going way. The entire stimulus has come from the teaching staff as a means of improving what we can offer to students.

(David Ibbotson)

Curriculum development must reflect the students' needs and future progress – it also needs to develop cohesively rather than piecemeal in a hundred different schools. I see no mileage in each establishment reinventing the wheel (i.e. devising courses when central planning can maintain national standards and opportunities).

(Yvonne Pickersgill)

Since coming out of mainstream teaching I feel my professionalism has been valued. I have had the freedom to really look at and assist in meeting the needs of the adults who come to us with literacy and numeracy problems. The other trainers and myself have been able to pool ideas and work together as a team, responding to situations as they arise and adopting a holistic approach rather than a subject orientated one.

(Sue Brooks)

'There is more scope post-16'

Much of the earlier curriculum development I was involved in was very prescriptive. National Curriculum requirements are very rigid. The

Youth Award Scheme and GNVQs are more flexible – they give a broader framework.

(Nicholas Bush)

I have taken a very proactive leading role, initiating a great deal of post 16 curriculum development, and have provided and delivered the INSET to support it. I feel that staff are becoming increasingly cynical and resistant to change. A great deal of resources have to be put into staff support and development if curriculum is to be successful.

(J. Barron)

On-going curriculum development has always been a foundation stone of good teaching practice. As a teacher in an 11–16 school, then a main grade lecturer in a college of FE, I was always responsive to new developments that enhanced learning. As a senior lecturer in FE with responsibility for school liaison, I worked very hard to develop initiatives that were about continuity and progression from pre-16 to post-16 education. Now, as Director of Curriculum Development for a college of FE, one of our biggest challenges comes from the impact of the FEFC funding methodology. Students must not only be recruited but be retained and achieve. If not, the lost revenue to the college is enormous. Curriculum development is therefore driven by guiding students on to the right courses and giving them a relevant quality curriculum that will enable them to succeed. Developments like the ASDAN Award Scheme will help colleges meet this challenge.

(K. Truman)

Ironically, as the level of prescription for teachers has increased, my career has moved me into a position to be able to exercise some autonomy, so I haven't felt the pinch as much as some. The post-16 picture is where there is still considerable scope for creativity and this has been my focus. I've had a free hand to experiment here with post-16 breadth and to introduce GNVQs as appropriate.

(Pam Taylor)

I have become much more involved with curriculum development work since I became Director of Sixth Form studies five years ago. More recently I have become involved in teaching GNVQ leisure and tourism, which has equipped me to teach core skills – relevant to the Youth Award Scheme.

(John Nunn)

I have more of a role now since the college incorporated the idea of free-standing core skills for students not on GNVQ/NVQ programmes, i.e. on GCSE and A level courses. I have been giving management staff information about ASDAN FE Award and assessing core skills. I am a lead tutor on the curriculum support team and have a role in the development of tutorial provision/guidance/support to students, and in the recording of achievement.

(Linda Chance)

There is more scope in FE: for example, writing GNVQ assignments and City & Guilds performing arts assignments.

(Phil Courage)

Originally I was a lecturer in physics and maths but now I coordinate a whole range of activities and have been developing the ASDAN programme across college. I have found it to be both stimulating and academically challenging, and the students have benefited from its introduction.

(Lesley Harrison)

'We are in danger of excluding pupils from this process'

As someone who made a career out of research and now teaching I value the importance of learning immensely. It is clear to me, however, that we are in danger of excluding pupils from this process by rewarding those who achieve only the highest attainment levels. For the majority of pupils in our school this is simply not a realistic target. If we are to educate all pupils we need to widen the routes into education and not place insurmountable barriers in their way. Learning is a lifelong process and we should be aware of our responsibilities in ensuring this continues. Over reliance on one academic route is bound to create 'casualties' and this underclass is much in evidence in our school.

(Geoffrey Osborn)

The revised curriculum has allowed for flexibility, especially in Key Stage 4. We may eventually achieve the balance that was present before which did not necessarily force less able pupils down an examination route, but recognized the need to have a variety of alternatives. Teachers are more accountable which is a good thing, but it is difficult to always succeed in trying to get new ideas in place, as people are frightened to experiment since they are always looking at the performance related league tables.

(Shelley Reddan)

When GCSE came out they were supposedly the be all and end all, and cover the whole ability range. Many schools are seeking a course which will provide suitable motivation and accreditation for those who cannot cope with GCSEs. What a surprise!

(Liz Towers)

I have long believed that school is about much more than just academic qualifications. The many contributions that pupils make to the school community are being recognised through the Youth Award Scheme. They are also having self esteem enhanced by being given credit for 'day to day' achievements that previously received no recognition.

(John Nunn)

In special education of all kinds one has to deal with the whole child, not merely its academic levels. The pressures of national curriculum mean that either we cannot now deal with the problems of the child adequately, or we cannot teach the National Curriculum to its full extent. As it happens we tend to fall between both stools – to the detriment of the children.

(Colin Whittaker)

My main concern is for the ever increasing 'out of school' population – students who have a lot to offer society but have been let down by the education system. Why are schools not engaging these students? With the existence of league tables, more youngsters are going to be thrown out of mainstream and this will have an impact if something isn't done soon.

(Che Hill)

THE STATUS OF TEACHERS AS PROFESSIONALS

Question 3: Could you offer comments, reflecting your own views, about the status of teachers as professionals, and how this may (or may not) have changed over the years you've been a teacher?

'Status – what's that?'

I feel very saddened by the overall self-esteem of teachers. New teachers have so much content to get through in their subjects that they very rarely feel able to experiment with different approaches which may make learning more effective for all involved. I believe that the atmosphere has become one of uncertainty and mistrust and this must have a knock-on effect for all involved. I also feel very angry at having so many outside agencies coming in and offering yet more advice, or new and more paperwork.

(Karen Jenkins)

The status of teachers is much lower these days. The community's confidence, respect and trust in teachers has been undermined by changing social attitudes and economic climate; also undermined by political attacks since 1985 – a punishment by the government for industrial action – hence such things as excessive concentration on parents' rights and expectations, without confirmation of parental responsibilities and accountability.

(Ivan Prokaza)

I feel the status has deteriorated dramatically since I entered the profession. I find that the pupils have little respect, especially for junior members of staff, who find the situation difficult to deal with. I also feel that teachers are not prepared well enough for the rigours of teaching today, which leads to staff sometimes not being as professional as they should be. Parents also regard teachers as 'lowly beings', which does not help the pupil attitudes.

(A. Hoodless)

I previously worked as a probation officer, so I feel my professional status dropped when I moved into education . . . We are trying to be planners, accountants, business forecasters, and so on, which dissipates our energies.

(Maureen Wilsdon)

The status has diminished over the past 20 years, partly because of frequent public criticism, such as lowering standards, but also as a result of teachers themselves. Widespread action in the 1980s did not help, but newcomers these days seem less committed in terms of time they're willing to give, or responsibilities assumed before more remuneration is sought.

(Susan Summers)

When I started to teach I thought I knew my subject and strengths. By 1989 the whole situation had changed and it was embarrassing to admit socially that you were a teacher.

(Judith Harwood)

Teachers have been their own worst enemies for not insisting on a proper professional council. However, the most awful aspect of teaching has been watching morale drop and each time thinking it can't get any lower. It can. It has.

(Mike Carver)

There seems to be a lack of trust and respect from the political arena and no longer can what teachers say be taken at face value. There are arguments to support this (poor teachers), but much has been destroyed in the over simplistic approach that has been adopted towards education. Groups of teachers from different schools rarely meet now to discuss good practice – we are in competition!

(Graham Wright)

Teacher status has been eroded. Most messages from all political parties focus on the shortcomings of the profession rather than the high quality work that is the norm in nearly all schools.

(S. Bull)

We have less status than 22 years ago when I first qualified, and less support from other colleagues. 'Dog eat dog' is more or less the status quo these days. LMS has divided my town and there is no longer inter-school support.

(Anon)

The status in the eyes of the community and pupils in general has gone down. What is shown on TV and in papers often belittles or blames teachers, and there are very few students whom I meet looking at teaching as a career compared to even seven years ago. On a personal note, I get letters of thanks and even the odd bouquet which is encouraging. But best of all the students keep in contact and I can see their progress.

(Gill Noel)

Status – what's that? During the past few years my position as a teacher/
senior manager has become eroded by a variety of things: government's
attitude to us as professionals – setting up a system of teaching that is
only suitable for the majority not the whole range, then criticizing us
when we fail to achieve appropriate levels at KS4; the press who love
the gossip when schools/teachers fail – when it's often due to lack of
resources/appropriate training/class sizes/type of catchment and so on;
ourselves being willing (too willing?) to cooperate and try to establish new
ideas and systems, which turn out to be impossible (How many versions
of the National Curriculum have there been? What weight of paperwork
did we have before the government decided to streamline it?); our unions/
professional bodies who have been sucked in to what the government
proposes because we are afraid of criticism from parents; our governors,
who generally are untrained and not prepared for the role.

(Kiri Garbut)

In the popular press teachers enjoy low esteem and always have done in
my experience. This reflects the widespread conception of short hours,
long holidays and such like. Ofsted's 15,000 failing teachers hasn't helped.
The status of teachers continues to be reflected in the relatively low
salary.

(Keith Hutt)

Work load and expectations have increased steadily. But status and recognition have been on a continued downward trend. I don't feel teachers
are regarded as professionals in any sense by the public or politicians.

(Margaret Tucker)

'Parental support has definitely changed'

Status as seen by both pupils and parents has dropped greatly. However
in the independent sector this is not as large a problem as in the state
sector (I have taught in both). Could parental views and back up have
anything to do with this?

(M. Walker)

Parental support has definitely changed. In turn this has had a knock-
on effect on pupil attitudes. Teachers are no longer regarded as the
'expert' – our views are regularly challenged.

(Gwyn Evans)

Amongst parents, politicians and the general public I feel that teachers
have a low professional status. Those closely connected to teachers and
teachers themselves are only too well aware of the hard work and dedi-
cation shown by most teachers, especially so during the last two decades
when the demands have been greatest.

(Martin Wilcox)

It's changed vastly. I have given up a pastoral role (deputy head of lower
school) with no regrets – basically because I am so tired of having to

justify every move to parents who don't support us. The government has pushed more and more on to us, for less and less pay and the 'knocking' from them has transferred to the community. We are not respected any more.

(Anon.)

When I started in pastoral care in the late 1960s parents asked for advice and appreciated any help the school gave. By the time I moved from pastoral care last year parents expected me to provide solutions and take responsibility for their son/daughter's behaviour in and out of school!

(Mary Brennan)

In 1972 teachers were respected for the job they did by parents and students. Their opinions on subject matter was also considered. Today the respect and value put on their professional opinions has diminished in some areas.

(J. Marsh)

Whilst accountability of teachers has increased, there has been little (as yet) accountability for the other 'partners' in the educational process.

(J. Jones)

'Professional judgement counts for little'

I come from an academic university background and have been teaching for nearly three years. My impression is that my professional judgement counts for very little. What I teach is prescribed and how I assess pupils' performance is judged unsatisfactory given the amount of external testing forced upon the profession. Furthermore, school performance is determined by a narrow band of statistical indicators (percentage A–Cs) with little recognition given to the starting point of pupils. I work in a very demanding school and have never worked harder in my life. It galls me that no matter what I do these efforts and those of the vast majority of pupils that I teach will remain unrecognised under the present system of measuring school performance. In return I am berated by the Ofsted inspectorate and accused of having low standards of achievement and expectation for my pupils. I suspect my own standing in the eyes of the public will improve only when I decide to move to a more 'successful' academically achieving school. Some reward for following one's convictions!

(Geoffrey Osborn)

Within the profession there is more 'professionalism' than ever before, a greater time commitment, and more 'care' for pupils. However, there is a progressive decline in the respect shown by other professionals, and certainly less regard by the pupils than ever before. There is more and more questioning of 'why', which has increased continually since National Curriculum introduction.

(H. Bowles)

Teachers used to be trusted to deliver a curriculum which suited the needs of their intake. That has gradually been eroded; now we receive a rap over the knuckles if we stray away from GCSE courses. What has happened? We now have a developing truancy problem as GCSE does not suit at least one-third of our children. This is not being defeatist, it is being a realist.

(John Bament)

We are no longer credited with being capable of making decisions about the best way to educate children, but have most decisions imposed by the government. The introduction of modern foreign language for all is a classic example. In 1970, I decided how and what to teach my pupils, with guidance and support from management and LEA.

(Penelope Rea)

I feel that we are increasingly devalued as professionals, at times by the larger educational system but also at times by the hierarchy within individual schools. Resources have a great deal to do with this. Giving people confidence and professional autonomy is expensive. Teachers are not always valued by others outside the profession who do not understand the constraints. There are too many parents who are prepared to defend their rights without thinking about their responsibilities. Pupils also question the professional approach of teachers.

(J. Barron)

I feel that over the last few years the teaching profession has been able to hold its head high at the way it has responded to new government initiatives. So much has been thrown at us and we have taken it all on board, with a minimum of resources and very little extra time or money. Most teachers are very professional people and do care about their pupils.

(Philippa Wadsworth)

Teachers are, of course, highly skilled council workers. There is a lot of snobbery around about 'professionalism'. I think we are seen by the current government as a problem species. Curriculum guidance is valued when it is offered by those with a background which is not an educational one. Teachers' views are thus marginalized.

(Pete Whalen)

I have been teaching for 31 years. One concern is that major initiatives are now top down, which is a reflection on how teachers are viewed. For example, the move to terminal assessment in GCSEs seems to suggest that teachers are not sufficiently professional to work a package based on continuous assessment.

(John Edwards)

'Professional autonomy has mostly disappeared'

It is time the government allowed teachers to do what they know best: they don't tell solicitors and doctors how to follow their professions.

Leave us alone! Stop the media filling people's heads with criticism of things such as trendy methods.

(Myra Levine)

The 'professional autonomy' of teachers has mostly disappeared. We are not professionals because we haven't the time and resources necessary to allow us to think about what we are doing. Surely the work of a professional is someone who practises, trains, analyses their 'job' as well as performs it. Yearly we do more with less and are forced to perform to dictated agendas. It's ironic, because we teachers know that the best development isn't dictated, it's achieved by those who 'own' it.

(Ivan Prokaza)

I consider education to be a running sore which will not improve until our masters cease from playing with it. A long and sustained period of stability is required, where the onus is once again shifted onto the professional to make the best use of the tools available.

(Mark Read)

For a brief spell of five years TVEI gave schools and teachers time and money in which to carry out curriculum development. Unfortunately that initiative has passed and once more we are expected to develop, be innovative, produce materials, record and report (in whose time?) as well as carry out the hundred other tasks expected by government.

(Martin Wilcox)

Apart from the Award Scheme and our Link Course, I have very little professional autonomy. I have to deliver a prescribed curriculum in both English and GNVQ. I have little opportunity to exercise my professional judgement about what pupils need. I have to deliver their 'entitlement' – whether it is appropriate or not.

(Liz Parker)

I do remember CSE Mode 3 (vaguely!) and I do feel that there is much less autonomy as the degree of accountability has increased, together with the need to justify and record all activities. There seems to be less time and space for the 'hidden curriculum' as we all expend so much effort, not just 'doing' but recording what we do.

(Jane Williams)

'The future of our children depends on enthusiasm and adventure within schools'

Teachers must be allowed the opportunity for professional autonomy and responsibility. If the professional integrity of teachers is continually undermined, we will eventually end up with a very stagnant, boring and unenthusiastic teaching 'profession'. The future of our children depends on some sparks of enthusiasm and adventure with schools.

(J. Barron)

I think teachers today are more hard-working and more professional than they have ever been before – there is now far more discussion of what we do and how best we can do it. Therefore I believe teachers are better equipped to handle the autonomy they once enjoyed, but which is now largely denied them.

(Dr Richard Gurnham)

The Youth Award Scheme works because it depends upon a collective definition and understanding of the spirit of the thing. Once you've got that it guides you through interpretations of the 'rules'. Non-teacher led development doesn't have that because either none of us know what the spirit is supposed to be or it's not our idea, so we've no investment in making it work. Almost all queries about standards can be answered by reference to the 'feel' of a scenario rather than by reference to subsection 4 paragraph 3. I suppose I'm saying curriculum development and professional autonomy are linked, and I'm sure Michael Fullan's work would back me up if I were to look up the reference!

(Kath Grant)

I wish we could be left alone to develop the curriculum that we would like to provide and stop trying to keep us as second class grammar schools. Most creative curriculum development costs money.

(Ian Booth)

I am completing this the day after the terrible incident in Dunblane. Mr Major made a comment last night. It went something like 'sympathy to the families . . . and the teachers who will cope with the result of this event'. This sums up the profession – we will cope with whatever we are asked to do. Parents, employers, politicians all criticize teachers but they know they can rely on us to do what is necessary in any situation.

(Mary Brennan)

To value the 'teaching relationship', the commitment and inspiration which great teachers so freely give to their students, would be to acknowledge what is good in our education system, and to celebrate the great hope for our children's future.

(Frank Byle)

'Teaching seems to have been forced into second place'

Even though still relatively inexperienced and only really knowing this particular way of doing things, I still feel aggrieved that we spend so long justifying and recording all that we do and are not really able to get on and concentrate on teaching the children as effectively as possible. Nothing is left to interpersonal skills and professional ability.

(David Lewis)

Since I started teaching, the work load and what is expected of us has increased enormously. All pupils have to be entered for outside examinations, which makes us much more accountable for the pupils' attainments.

(F. Langford)

The National Curriculum has sharpened the focus of the teacher but has equally become so labour intensive with all the recording that has to go on. I spend far too much time completing records and charts at the expense of preparing pupil materials.

(Shelley Reddan)

Increased administration and bureaucracy have taken teachers away from the job they do best – teaching children.

(Neil Judges)

There is much less ownership of the curriculum. New courses leave little scope for creativity or even adaptability to local conditions. Teachers are 'trainers' delivering preset courses to preset standards. Financial constraints mean lecturers no longer have time allocated for 'enrichment' experiences, such as residentials, tutorials and other marginal activities.

(Bette Liddell)

Teachers have been swamped with administration and paperwork. Teaching seems to have been forced into second place and paper work the all important goal. I feel the priorities have been placed wrongly. When I started teaching, work with the children was what was important – today it seems to be record keeping and writing of schemes of work, lesson plans and so on.

(Colin Whittaker)

The teaching profession has been faced with so many changes over the last few years that the profession as a whole feels undervalued by both parents and the government. The joy of teaching, the giving of information and sharing knowledge seem to be things of the past.

(Che Hill)

'Teacher bashing is now a national sport'

I think our status is lower now. The government and the mass media always criticize us – highlighting failure and ignoring success. Teacher-bashing is now a national sport. Most of my colleagues would leave teaching if they had the chance. I feel undervalued and overworked.

(Liz Parker)

Since the government has been taking a more prescriptive role in education, the general public seem to think they now know what should or should not be done in education. The position of teachers has been undermined and they seem to be the scapegoats for all society's problems.

(Vicki Ponsford)

Society seems to blame teachers for all sorts of things and expect them to put them right. Parents' responsibility seems to have waned.

(Howard Bell)

The status of teachers has declined as they have increasingly been held responsible for problems caused by society's ills. They have been forced to become commercial managers and pushed into a market place mentality which has detracted from their role as educators.

(Elaine Lowe)

Teachers are not treated as professionals by the government or the media. 'Let's bash the teachers' is good to detract attention from failing policies and makes good headlines. Over the years, there has been constant erosion of status – reflected in monitoring and frequent inspections. What is needed is less paperwork and more time to devote to relevant work.

(Anna Roberts)

When I first started teaching that is all I was expected to do by parents, children and my superiors. Now we are asked to be social workers, religious teachers, sex educators and moral guiders. It seems parents are no longer willing or able to take responsibility for their own children and when anything goes wrong we are to blame. I suppose everyone needs a scapegoat.

(Jacalin Chawner)

Teacher bashing seems to be the norm – we are blamed for all the ills of modern society from vandalism to unemployment. Parents and pupils all seem to know their 'rights' when it comes to education, but very few realize that 'rights' and 'responsibilities' are partners.

(Sheila Knight)

'The most rewarding job possible'

I started teaching in 1985. I feel that during the following few years teacher status within society plummeted. However, public opinion is beginning to become favourable towards teachers again with a realization of the conditions we are now having to face (such as inadequate funding, large class sizes and redundancies).

(Nicholas Bush)

Status has changed as society's perception of authority has changed. However, what has happened is that those who can't are increasingly being found out. The dictatorial (mainly lazy) staff I first worked with now hardly exist. Most of us are overworked and stressed but the best still find it the most rewarding job possible.

(Ian Booth)

I began teaching during the action of 1984/5 when Mode 3 was being rubbished and Thatcher was starting the Great Education Reforms, so I was under few illusions about teacher status. My personal perception is that we're starting to move back up the status ladder in response to the government moving down the popularity stakes. In some ways people entering teaching from other routes (e.g. industry) have boosted us by recognizing that it's not all holidays and then circulating this new perception in their non-teaching networks.

(Kath Grant)

I started teaching when the teachers' action was at its height. I think our status (and morale) was at its lowest then. Since 1987 I have felt an increase in morale overall – although it is still very low and there's a feeling of entrenchment within the teachers' own concept of professionalism. I think public perception of teachers has improved overall and there is grudging recognition of the work load, stress and commitment of teachers. Equally we have seen a new breed of teachers brought up on a diet of constant change, and therefore more resilient to it, whilst at the same time we have lost hundreds of excellent teachers who couldn't cope – mostly in the older bracket.

(Clive Baker)

I think that my school has adopted a far more professional approach to teaching than twenty years ago when I first started. There has been a great effort made to end the separation of pastoral and academic aspects. This entails a much greater workload.

(N. Smith)

I feel the profession has become more rigorous. For all the faults in the changes, and the lack of funding and resources I feel that there is some value in being made more accountable and more aware of quality control.

(C. Morrish)

I think our standing as professionals has increased with the greater accountability we now face. Although we've always worked hard and now we're working harder, at least we've got a framework to work to and we're not reinventing the wheel all the time. Now we can put our energies into other areas.

(Wendy Chandler)

It's a wonderful job – mostly because of the constant change. Now I have an MA. Then I had a Cert Ed – does this reflect professionalism or bullshit?

(Dave Simmons)

'And as for money . . .'

Houghton seemed to be the only body which really valued teachers. Part of the trouble is that the profession tends to be regarded as a homogeneous entity when the characteristics of the job – from nursery to FE – can be very different. I feel that my present job is as rewarding as I am likely to get and I look back in horror at the stresses of 17 years in Inner London schools. But Inner London was an authority which cared and put its money where its mouth was. It also introduced a system of inspection and support which hasn't been bettered. So it had to go. Frequently teachers in more stressful institutions are regarded as less competent and less effective simply because they are unable to compensate for inadequacies of parenthood, peer pressures, media and society demands, and such like. And that is without the progressive withdrawal of funding and support for the social services, so that, more and more, schools are expected to compensate.

Degradation of teachers began long ago. Kenneth Baker didn't exactly help when he imagined he would make the system more effective by measuring it. From then on, teachers were not to be trusted to organise their own time. 1265 hours were to be demanded. There were doubtless fruitful spin-offs from this but for many staff that was the end of Saturday morning supervision of sports and other voluntary activities; they thought, 'Stuff it if we're not going to be valued.' I think that marked a sea change in attitudes and levels of commitment. I believe that it is not simply coincidental that many complain of the deterioration in the levels of state school sports.

About this time the other thing to knock was the quality of teachers. But the government was going to do something about this. Yes, siree, they were going to make sure that the profession would in the near future become all-graduate. That, of course, was when there was a bit of money in the coffers. Then it changed. Now the main qualifications are that you need a bit of interest, can speak a modicum of English, and don't mind learning on the job.

Then along came the National Curriculum. Not because it is of intrinsic value to pupils, but because politicians can keep a closer eye on teachers and pretend that they, the politicians, are doing something useful and measurable. And they can construct neat and tidy league tables which put nice middle class schools at the top and demonstrate that inner city schools – mostly in Labour-controlled boroughs – are crap. Concepts of value added were trendy and, of course, to be ignored. Fortunately they were unable to stifle *all* of the outcry and modifications and a few changes of policy have taken place.

CPVE came and went and then we moved into acronymical megadrive. NCVQ, NVQ, BTEC, and so on – mostly designed for post-school and post-16, but filtered downwards because in the certificate quagmire there was precious little to inspire low achievers. D34 and D35 have entered the teaching vocabulary as verbs. What sort of communicators have we become? Then, just as we are beginning to work out what the letters mean they change. One minute A levels are the gold standard, then there is to be a parallel and more practical route. Then AS entered and is now clearly on the way out. Then we hear that GNVQ standards are so low that the scheme may change. And now the whole of the A level route may change again, and the merry-go-round continues.

The system wasn't satisfactory. So let's persuade industry to cough up for specialist city technology schools, outside of the state system, to provide examples of good practice. But industry wasn't that gullible and the government ended up pouring in millions of desperately needed pounds into a crackpot scheme, short-changing local authority schools in the process. Now all government talk of CTCs has gone terribly muted.

Meanwhile other schools crumble. So how about offloading them? Bribe them to opt out. Few were that daft; logic dictated that a short-term windfall was not likely to last. So instead we get local management of schools and colleges. This has its merits, but the price we pay is that the idea of a regional policy for education goes out of the window. Support centres have disappeared and the dominant ethos is now competition, not cooperation. The prevailing language is management-speak, with marketing challenges, franchise opportunities, curricular niches, and so on.

And quality control. Yes that matters. So we'll inspect. Every four years. According to Our Criteria. And cheaply. So we advertise for bids. And so it came to pass. If it is not cheap it shall be efficient. And if it is not efficient it shall be cheap. The result? Not the improvement of teacher skills or educational planning by making recommendations and sending in teams of advisers. That would cost money. No. The outcome shall be a Grade, and that Grade shall be incorporated into League Tables. And then the market will do the rest. The trouble is inspectors don't seem to want to do the job and the shortfall is such that ideas of four-yearly cycles seem to be fading fast.

Meanwhile in Scotland, where more than 95 per cent of the student population have gone to comprehensive schools since the early 1960s, there has been significantly less tinkering. Exam results are higher than in England, as are perceptions of the quality of education being received. It's not the system as much as the stability which matters. And that is something which we certainly don't have. It's driving many out of the profession and others into an early grave. And that isn't exaggerating the problem. And as for money . . .

(Jim Harnes)

eight _____

The ASDAN Award Scheme: a case study of teacher-led curriculum development

INTRODUCTION

The Award Scheme Development and Accreditation Network (ASDAN) is a remarkable curriculum phenomenon of the 1980s and 1990s.

Devised, initiated, implemented and organized entirely by the profession, it now operates in one-third of the secondary schools in England and Wales, with over 120,000 young people in the 14–19 age group registered for various levels of the award. It straddles the pre- and post-16 experience of students by offering a progressive series of awards at Bronze, Silver, Gold and Platinum (Universities) levels. To achieve each level young people are encouraged to complete assignments from a menu of challenges within 'areas of activity' that include international relations, world of work, the community, economic and industrial affairs, science and technology, expressive arts, health and survival, information handling, the environment, industry and technology, home management, and sport and leisure. This whole suite of awards provides a 'curriculum enrichment' programme in its own right, as well as a mechanism for assessing and accrediting key/core skill competence at NCVQ related levels 1 to 4.

In 1985 the Award Scheme was running in just one school in one LEA. By 1996, 1830 schools and colleges in 84 LEAs were registered for various levels of the award scheme, with the Universities and Colleges Admissions Service highlighting the significance of the award in its guidance notes to schools and colleges relating to university entrance (UCAS 1996).

As Chapter 5 illustrates, there have been a number of other important curriculum initiatives for the 14–19 age group in the past ten years. In addition to GCSE, the GNVQ is perhaps the most well known, with 200,000 students registered for the various levels. Alongside this, BTEC, CGLI, RSA and other awarding bodies accredit a range of courses, and programmes like

Project Trident, Young Enterprise and Crest Awards have been introduced in a large number of schools (Crombie White *et al.* 1995).

However, when the history of curriculum development in the closing decades of the twentieth century is written up at an appropriate point in the future, the ASDAN Award Scheme is likely to stand apart from all the others, distinguished by certain factors that make it unique. Its uniqueness and its success generate a number of fascinating questions.

For instance, how is it that one teacher's idea for enhancing the extra-curricular experience of students in a south Devon comprehensive in the early 1980s has become transformed into the largest national programme for accreditation of 'core skills' alongside GNVQs? How has this happened without on-going development funds from the large examination boards or from statutory bodies like SCAA or the Department of Employment? And how is it that in an era when curriculum development is increasingly becoming centrally directed and controlled, with millions being spent on glossy brochures and advertising, schools and colleges are signing up in their hundreds for an initiative that largely relies on 'word of mouth' for its publicity?

There have been no 'national launches', no centre page feature advertisements in the educational press and no interviews with BBC presenters on *Today*. Yet each year the take-up of the scheme has continued along an exponential curve. In seeking explanations for this phenomenon and drawing out lessons from a study of this initiative, we need to make reference to the changing context of curriculum development in England and Wales, alongside the notion of professional autonomy, as outlined in the early chapters of this book. You may find it useful, at stages, to turn back to appropriate pages, to set the story of the Award Scheme within the wider canvas of the national picture of curriculum change.

GERMINATION OF AN IDEA: THE AWARD SCHEME IN DEVON 1982–7

Do you recall the educational scene in the autumn of 1982?

LEAs controlled most of the things that affected schools: admissions policies, capitation, appointments of headteachers and senior staff, curriculum policies, staff development.

Local management of schools had yet to be invented. Although frustrated headteachers may often have wished a thunderbolt could strike down the bureaucrats in 'county halls' who seemed to obstruct every creative idea, there was no possibility of 'opting out'. The introduction of the Assisted Places Scheme the year before had created some consternation among comprehensive schools in the proximity of any of the independent schools to be favoured with such funding, but mostly people were reassured that it was intended for the 'deserving poor'.

The Schools Council was still flourishing. Nancy Trenaman's Review of 1981 had reported very favourably on its work in the light of evaluations that demonstrated how some projects had 'radically altered teachers' classroom practice, improving tremendously the quality of learning by pupils' (Truman 1985). The future looked promising.

Keith Joseph, who'd replaced Mark Carlisle as Secretary of State for Education, was adamant that there was no need to legislate for a national curriculum, and seemed more concerned about the plight of the 'bottom 40 per cent'. Records of Achievement and the Lower Attaining Pupils Programme had been announced as measures to boost the performance of this group.

Extra-curricular activities were a regular feature of school life. Most teachers willingly donated hours of time to run clubs and supervise activities at lunch times and after school. The teacher 'action' that was to put on hold this aspect of the curriculum was several years away.

It was at this point that I met Brian Fletcher for the first time.

Following publication of *In and Out of School* (White and Brockington 1978), the Schools Council had agreed to fund a dissemination programme to promote the 'social and community education' ideas espoused in the book (Pring *et al*. 1982). Between 1980 and 1982 a series of regional conferences were staged around the UK. One of these, in Exeter in 1981, led to the setting up of a 14–18 curriculum working party chaired by Richard Pring at Exeter University. The principal aim of the group was to share and spread 'good practice' among the participating schools and colleges in Devon.

Concurrently a local trust was persuaded to make £2000 available for assisting with the development of selected initiatives. I had the job of sharing out the funds, which meant visiting each of the schools involved. The deputy head of one of the Exeter schools, Brian Fletcher, had invited me in to discuss an idea for curriculum enrichment. He had constructed his own 'award scheme' to offer accreditation to his fourth and fifth year groups for a whole range of achievements that weren't recognized within the traditional examination framework. In his school in Exeter twenty of the team of sixty staff were involved in organizing, supporting, assisting and assessing those pupils who had elected for the award scheme as an extra-curricular activity. About half of each year group was registered with the scheme, which pupils saw as relevant to their perceived needs.

Brian met me in reception and took me round the school. It was sometime later that I learnt he'd stood as parliamentary candidate for the Plymouth Drake constituency in October 1974. After five recounts the result was announced, with Brian 34 votes short of victory. The loss to Parliament was education's gain. Sometimes you find yourself in the presence of people who convey a sincerity and conviction that runs deeper than mere words. That afternoon was such a moment for me as Brian enthused about the award scheme. 'It's not a question of passing or failing; it's about rewarding success,' he explained. 'I want to encourage a variety of activities and I need a base where the students can do things.' The emphasis was on the word 'do', and Brian needed equipment for the 'base' – a project workshop which would provide pupils with access to work surface, hand tools and storage.

The Schools Council project was able to contribute £700, which pump-primed the raising of the additional monies needed to complete the workshop. That same year the award scheme was written into the school curriculum as an option for the first time. Fifty pupils elected to take up the scheme.

And then the Technical and Vocational Education Initiative (TVEI) was announced in November 1982. The history and impact of this programme has been well documented by others (Dale *et al.* 1990; Gleeson and McLean 1994; Williams and Yeomans 1994). Administered by the Manpower Services Commission, whose chairman was David Young, it was intended to spread the 'infection of technical education more widely through all our schools' (BBC 1983). Although in the *Times Educational Supplement* at the time David Young was 'wickedly caricatured as a burglar, making off with our children's precious education' (BBC 1983), TVEI had the full support of the Secretaries of State for Education and Employment (Keith Joseph and Norman Tebbit respectively), as well as the Prime Minister. Keith Joseph was at pains to stress that it 'is only a pilot scheme, which has the full backing of the LEAs.'

Exeter was one of the first wave of 14 consortia of schools to be funded by this pilot, and Brian's school took advantage of the funding to extend the award scheme within the framework of the personal and community services curriculum. Indeed, the TVEI pilot itself drew heavily on good award scheme practice, and other schools in the Devon area expressed interest in aspects of the scheme. The badges and certificates that St Thomas High School had produced for different levels of the scheme were sought after by others, including participants at the 1983 National Organisation for Initiatives in Social Education (NOISE) conference, at which Brian agreed to discuss the award framework. Brian Fletcher and his colleague Nigel Way ran workshops on the Exeter Award Scheme at the annual NOISE conference for three years (Fletcher 1983; Way 1985). Their groups were always oversubscribed and there was a lot of talk of developing the scheme within other schools. It felt time to grasp the nettle and produce the materials in a format that others could use.

With funding support from Television South West (TSW) and the Gulbenkian Foundation, a video-led teacher's pack was prepared about the award scheme. It contained guidelines for tutors, together with copies of the workbooks for use by pupils at the various levels. The video offered a case study commentary over a sequence of slides that illustrated the award scheme in action.

The TSW Youth Award Scheme offers a range of practical activities which encourage personal, social and educational development. This often involves going out of school, frequently working unsupervised.

Pupils are provided with the opportunity to succeed, which is an important factor in helping to improve their self image.

The original aims of the scheme are to develop confidence, social competence and a range of practical skills, through learning activities based firmly in the community. With the co-operation of teaching staff, community workers and local employers, pupils learn in and out of school following their own individualised timetable.

When certificates first began to be awarded for achievement the response from pupils was tremendous. They thrived on success and being rewarded for it.

So the Award Scheme emerged. It lays a structure for the areas of activity and awards certificates for achievement. It allows pupils to succeed by selecting their own tasks and completing them at their own pace; it is open to all pupils in the school and offered as a part of their timetabled curriculum.

(Brockington and White 1986)

Ten years on the video itself seems like the product of amateurish enthusiasm. However, within a year of its publication, 300 copies had been sold and reports were coming in from schools interested in incorporating its ideas within their curriculum. The phone was beginning to ring from schools wanting advice on practical matters to do with implementation. Many of them were using TVEI money for pump-priming local developments, drawing on the model promoted in the Exeter pilot.

By the time the video pack was completed Brian Fletcher had taken up a post as headteacher of Coombeshead School in Newton Abbot in Devon. In the same year that Brian obtained his headship I joined the staff at what was to become the University of the West of England, with one of the few faculties of education in the UK to achieve ratings of excellence. Geoff Whitty was the inspirational dean, who succeeded in doubling the size of the faculty within five years. His encouragement of curriculum and course development led to the setting up of a one-year short course for teachers interested in developing 'pre-vocational programmes' in schools and colleges. For the assessed assignment at the end of the course, it was intended that each participant would produce a practical suggestion for appropriate curriculum development in his or her establishment.

The story of the course itself offers an interesting mirror of national developments and how these affected schools at the time. In 1986 the course was oversubscribed. We could have filled the available places twice over from within schools in the Avon area. Teachers were eager to grasp the challenge of the pre-vocational developments and engage with practical curriculum initiatives. For the first two years the final assignments in almost every case informed related curriculum innovation in respective establishments. Teachers were coming on the course with a clear brief from their faculties or from senior management to address particular issues. By the fourth year of the course, in 1990, things had changed. The group size had shrunk, and the proposals for assignments were more tentative – either more narrowly focused on specific subject areas or generally more abstract in considering the wider 'issues' confronting the school. It was less clear that any recommendations would be implemented.

In the early days of the course, though, the enthusiasm to examine innovative practice was infectious. An annual highlight of the course and a major focus of professional interest was a visit to study the award scheme development at Coombeshead School and the other schools in the local consortium. This 'away day' in a coach to the depths of rural Devon in the first year of the course, in the spring of 1987, ended with beer and sandwiches in the White Hart in Exeter. Anyone who knows this pub will recall its wonderful wisteria. To walk into its cobbled courtyard in early May with the afternoon sunshine dappling the stone statues through the iridescent blueness of the blossom is to be transported into the essence of one aspect of Englishness. As the twenty of us from Bristol sat with our glasses and food in the warmth of the courtyard or in the heavy oak shade of the tap rooms, it wasn't surprising that imaginations began to run riot.

'What if . . .' and 'How could we . . . ?' and 'Where would we find funding . . . ?' were just some of the questions that floated around the group. In the coach on the way back ideas crystallized and the next meeting of the group resolved to establish a consortium of partner schools in Avon, with the aim of having something 'up and running' for the autumn term.

Coincidentally (are such things ever just coincidence?), I was approached by a BBC producer friend, Ian Woolf, who had been commissioned to do a number of films for the prestigious *Education Programme* series. He was looking for interesting examples of teacher led curriculum development: something creative; inspirational perhaps? Shakespeare got it in one with his 'There is a tide in the affairs of men' speech. We arranged to meet the following week. As the telephone clicked on to its rest I reached for my diary to check Brian Fletcher's number.

NURTURING YOUNG SHOOTS: THE EMERGENCE OF THE AVON AND BERKSHIRE AWARD SCHEME CONSORTIA 1987–90

The room in the Faculty of Education at Bristol Polytechnic was buzzing as the crew set up the lights. The selected core of teachers twisted nervously in their seats, joking about whether 'make up' was likely to arrive.

'Are you ready?' asked Ian Woolf.

The cameras rolled, taking in an hour of discussion among the teachers about the award scheme initiative they'd observed several weeks before at Coombeshead School. There were some remarkable contributions, drawing parallels between the scheme and Records of Achievement, linking it with the work of other initiatives such as TVEI and the Schools Curriculum Industry Partnership (SCIP), highlighting the underpinning educational principles . . . and all of it animated and intense and professional.

Four months later the film was screened on the *Education Programme* in October 1987, following a short clip about that part of the Queen's Speech that heralded the Education Reform Act and the introduction of a national curriculum. Then Martin Young reassured viewers that it was back to 'the main item'.

> Over the years more and more employers have been saying that exam qualifications don't necessarily make you the best person for the job. Fewer than a third of employers surveyed by the Polytechnic of Wales thought that academic CSEs and O levels are even important. They say that they want school leavers to show initiative, work with minimum supervision, possess organisational skills, work in a team, and make their own decisions. But employers aren't alone in doubting the present exam system, there are also teachers who feel that the emphasis on academic achievement is misleading, even unfair. Dick Benson is one of them.

There on the screen was the room at the polytechnic, rekindling memories of that evening in June when passion had flowed freely among the twenty teachers sitting in front of the camera. One face was in close up:

At primary schools you walk in and there is lots of activity, it's fun learning, it's activity based . . . then for some strange reason they are expected to sit in silence for five or seven years and absorb all the rubbish that is being thrown towards them. Then their degree of success or not is measured by how many bits of paper they leave school with because they are asked to regurgitate all these facts, not skills, but facts, at the appointed hour on the appointed day. I don't think it's a very valuable way to assess the success of education.

He faded from the screen, and we watched Martin Young turn to the man beside him.

Brian Fletcher, as a headteacher, you've heard that man there saying there's rubbish being thrown at children sitting in rows. That's fairly strong stuff.

Brian demonstrated a hint of a smile.

I think he very much overstates the case and I think he denigrates what countless thousands of teachers have been trying to deliver through the curriculum for many years in an effective way . . . But there's an element of truth in the fact that if at 16 plus you sit all pupils down in a formal examination room and ask them to write about what they have learned in terms of knowledge, without assessing skills or experiences, then inevitably the teaching styles that will lead towards that is a formal one, is didactic, children sit in rows, and they don't learn the sort of skills that employers want in your survey from Wales.

Martin Young leaned forward. 'So you've pioneered an alternative to that?'

Yes we have. We've introduced into the curriculum what we call a Youth Award Scheme, which is really a programme in personal and social education that leads to totally new relationships between teachers and pupils . . . Parents have been very receptive to this scheme . . . and pupils find it highly motivating as they realise that these skills can't just be learnt in school completely, they have to mix with members of the community, go and talk to people, learn from people in the community, adults other than teachers, perhaps health visitors, JPs, doctors and so on.

'And that sort of skill is important to employers?' asked Martin Young. Brian nodded.

Very important to be able to organise your own time, to solve problems on your feet so to speak, when you phone someone up, and they are not there . . . and also to work with one another in a co-operative rather than a competitive way.

The film went on to celebrate the initiative that had taken root in the cluster of comprehensive schools in the Newton Abbot area.

The screening of the film catalysed considerable response from around the UK. It was clear it had tapped into an undercurrent of general concern among the teaching profession. The Devon consortium was able to send out copies of its curriculum materials, and the video-led teaching pack referred to earlier was also on offer.

Our focus, though, was still very much Bristol based. The group had agreed to develop a local consortium of participating schools during 1987–8, drawing on the materials already in use in Devon. It is a testimony to the cooperative spirit of those teachers already involved that there were no problems about copyright. No one 'laid claim' to ownership of the ideas or the materials. No-one's ego got in the way of the task that confronted us. There was just mutual exchange of experience and practice – a vivid illustration of the professionalism that characterizes teachers.

The Bristol cluster worked hard during the summer term to rewrite the programme for local consumption and to undertake some small scale pilots with selected young people. There were many out of hours meetings of small groups of the teachers involved, often in individual houses over a bottle of wine or a few beers. By the end of that term, booklets for the first two levels of the scheme and a staff handbook (Adams *et al.* 1987) were printed ready for use in the ten partner schools in the coming year.

What was less encouraging and what came as a big surprise to the group of teachers was the response from the LEA. One morning, shortly before the end of the summer term, I received a phone call from one of the award scheme coordinators, who'd been running a pilot with her leavers' group. She was upset and angry. 'We've got to stop doing youth awards. The head says the LEA won't back it. I don't know why.'

She promised to feed me more details as they emerged, and in the following days the picture became less blurred. It seemed that a circular letter had gone out to all the participating schools from the Director of Education, making it clear that the award scheme was not supported by the LEA. What had happened to prompt such a letter was a mystery for some days, but then various leaks and snippets of information that we collectively gathered enabled us to construct some sort of picture of events. Whether it was the full story or not we shall never know, because all our information was gleaned second hand.

It seemed there were objections from within 'county hall'. We understood that the impression being put around in some quarters was of a group of teachers intent on undermining county policy with regard to some of their own initiatives that overlapped with the award scheme. The particular irony here was that, out of a concern to embed the scheme as a county-wide development, representatives from the advisory service and these other areas of interest had been drawn into early discussions and meetings of the award scheme group. TRIST (TVEI Related In-service Training) had made an impact in Avon schools; Records of Achievements were coming on strong; work experience programmes were very active. There seemed all sorts of possibilities for mutual reinforcement between the various initiatives.

As a case study of power politics within an LEA, the events of the subsequent four months provide illuminating material. The episode is interesting for what it reveals about the whole issue of curriculum control, and the possibilities for tension between teacher-led curriculum development and LEA or national priorities. In this case a group of enthusiastic and committed teachers had come together to pilot a practical idea in response to a perceived need about aspects of personal and social education. In the tradition of the Schools Council they'd drawn on examples of 'good practice' from elsewhere and tailored the material for local consumption. The motivating force was coming from the schools themselves and the energies of individual teachers, yet the reaction of the local authority seemed obstructive and unsupportive, even when it was clear that this was something the headteachers of the partner schools were committed to. It was almost as if the LEA wished it would fail. If this sounds a bit far fetched it is probably worth noting that a very similar situation occurred in Devon in the early days of the award scheme development. Not only was Brian Fletcher reprimanded for having sent information about the scheme direct to the Chief Education Officer, but he was also called to account for the extent to which his initiative might undermine the Duke of Edinburgh's Award Scheme.

Arguably 1987 was not the best year to float the idea for yet another curricular initiative. And the following year was probably even worse as LEAs were struggling to come to terms with other consequences of the 1988 legislation, such as local financial management and formula funding of schools. Perhaps much of the problem was about bureaucracies and the limitations they inevitably impose on creative capacities.

How much of it, though, was to do with interpersonal rather than structural or organizational factors? Was it simply about status – that a group of comparatively junior teachers was pushing ahead with a curriculum initiative that clearly had wider implications? How much of the problem was down to bruised egos of some of the LEA personnel, who'd become used to being centre stage in terms of curriculum innovation, and found it difficult to reconcile themselves to the role of understudy? Was it simply that one or two individuals with access to the decision makers in the LEA offices were 'stirring it' out of pique?

The difficulty for the group of teachers in Avon was that they had limited access to the 'corridors of power'. In this respect, in the late 1980s, LEAs still exercised considerable control over the curriculum choices of schools. It was very difficult for ordinary teachers to penetrate the barriers that existed between their own classrooms and the offices of county hall. To find the time to correct misinformation and placate concerns was no mean feat, especially as the onus for resolving the problem was put on to the award scheme group. The events of that summer of 1987 would make interesting television drama.

Eventually, it *was* resolved, following a direct appeal to the Director of Education (which seemed to exacerbate the upset felt by some individuals), and the blocking letter from the LEA was rescinded early in the autumn term. The work continued and by the following summer term of 1988 the first students had completed respective levels of the award. HTV, the local television network, agreed to 'sponsor' an award ceremony, with coverage on the evening news slot. HTV was brilliant. It handled the publicity, laid on the refreshments, provided one of its star presenters, Richard Wyatt, to compere the evening and 'managed' the front of house for the night. It was a great evening for the staff and students involved. Richard Pring and Brian Fletcher both agreed to come along and say a few words, as did the Director of Education to do the presentations. Under the glare of camera lights, 40 students received certificates in front of their parents and friends. It felt as if the award scheme had finally arrived in the County of Avon.

The LEA was becoming much more supportive. Personalities changed; people left; there were new appointments. A development group was constituted with the support of Sue Plant, the adviser for personal and social education. Records of Achievement, Compact, work experience, careers service and 14–19 education were all represented, as was TVEI when Avon finally agreed to submit a bid late in the day. A new Director of Education also augured well for the project, with a 'strategic plan' that put the award scheme centre stage in the facilitation of 'progression' at 16 plus. At the third annual presentation of awards to 300 young people in the summer of 1990, his obvious enthusiasm for the work, and the opportunities it offered to schools, was a welcome breath of fresh air.

'Progression' and 'action planning' were two of the educational buzz phrases at that time, encouraged in part by the Training Agency, which had announced its intention the year before to invite bids to run 'youth development projects' (YDPs) around the country. The expectation was that these projects would explore the whole concept of 'individual action planning', with an eye on the NROVA (as the post-16 Record of Achievement was known – you may recall the grey 'pizza boxes' that generated much derision among the recipients).

The award scheme group submitted a YDP bid to enhance the work of the scheme in Avon and Devon, and to develop an additional consortium in Berkshire, where a lot of interest had been expressed after the *Education Programme* screening. The bid was approved – £132,000 over nearly three years. It was the first 'real' money the award scheme had secured, and it enabled us to negotiate several part-time secondments for key staff to undertake the intended development work. With Sue Plant's help it also pump-primed some additional support, via LEATGs money, in the form of a seconded teacher, Brian Hobbs, from Avon LEA.

In the subsequent two years the award scheme consolidated its position in the three counties. Considerable energies went into revising and rewriting the sets of student workbooks, establishing consortia groups along the lines of the old Mode 3 CSE groups, training and supporting staff in schools to run the scheme, developing resource packs to accompany the booklets, contributing to policy and planning meetings within the respective LEAs, talking with employers' groups and emerging school industry partnerships, such as Compact.

By the end of 1989 the materials had been trialled and tested. The feedback was very positive from the three consortia in Avon, Devon and Berkshire. It was time to 'go national'.

THE FLOWERING OF THE AWARD SCHEME: FROM LOCAL CURRICULUM INITIATIVE TO NATIONAL PROGRAMME 1990–6

February 1990 saw the core team waiting nervously in the foyer of the

Crest Hotel near Taunton. The display materials were neatly laid out in the conference room, the room was prepared for the 50 delegates, the video equipment and OHP had been tested. All we needed were the teachers to arrive.

This was to be the first of a series of ten national conferences planned for the spring and summer terms – with York, Liverpool, Cambridge, Birmingham, Bristol, London, Brighton, Burton upon Trent and Edinburgh as the venues for the other nine. Information about these conferences had been circulated to every secondary school and sixth form college in the country by national mailing. Some of the venues were booked up within weeks of the mailing.

Teachers started to arrive and we went through the usual pre-conference procedures – checking lists, handing out delegate packs, sorting problems over payment, responding to questions. The room filled up. Ten o'clock approached. Was our mounting apprehension similar to that experienced by bungee jumpers the second before they launch themselves off the top of whichever structure they're tied to?

Brian Fletcher had agreed to introduce the session. 'Good morning ... welcome ... congratulations to you all for making the time to be here ... our sincere hope is that we shall at least enable you to leave here feeling that the time was well spent.' It was a conference with a minimum of 'touchy-feely' exercises; not the sort where participants spend the morning in small groups with flip charts, discovering the collective expertise that enables them to address common concerns. The intention was that people would leave in a position to decide whether or not to take forward the scheme in their respective establishments.

The feedback from this conference was mostly very positive, and this experience was replicated in the other nine venues. The years after that first conference in Taunton saw the award scheme running workshops every term around the country, mostly in university faculties of education, which more closely correspond with the 'image' and 'mission statement' of the award scheme than the luxurious but neutral surroundings of hotel chains such as Forte Crest. Other regional consortia became quickly established as enthusiastic teachers and lecturers stepped forward to coordinate local developments.

In 1988 there were 25 schools and colleges involved; in 1990, 200 new centres had registered to run the award scheme; by 1993 it was 500 and, in September 1995, the figure was 1721. As this book goes to press more than 120,000 young people in the 14–19 age group are now engaged on one of the various levels of the different schemes on offer under the ASDAN umbrella. Almost every LEA in England and Wales is actively involved.

Feedback from the early pioneers resulted in revision of the materials on a kind of rolling remake that has been a feature of the award scheme's development. The programmes on offer expanded in response to consumer demand – to cater for the FE sector, special schools and adult training, in addition to the 14–18 age group in schools which is still the main focus of ASDAN's work.

By 1991 it became necessary to overlay a national structure on to the regional developments. The Award Scheme Development and Accreditation

Network (ASDAN) was officially formed and registered as a 'not for profit' company, and the coordinators in the regions around the UK came together for an action planning event that has now become an annual part of ASDAN's development.

Support at a national level has followed on from its success as a local initiative. Importantly for schools it is now listed on the DfEE's register of approved courses. For colleges there is financial significance attached to the various entries on FEFC Schedule 2A. In addition, UCAS has highlighted its significance on the Guidance for Applicants (UCAS 1996) and the CBI has endorsed its aims as being consonant with those espoused in documents such as *Towards a Skills Revolution* (1988) and *A Credit to Your Career* (1993). In 1996 ASDAN was granted awarding body status by NCVQ in relation to its capacity to develop and accredit core (now key) skills. The seedcorn that had been nurtured by those committed groups of teachers in Devon and Avon in the mid-1980s has finally emerged on the national scene as a major contributor to the implementation of 'curriculum enrichment' and the accreditation of key skills.

EXPLANATIONS FOR THE SUCCESS OF THE ASDAN AWARD SCHEME: THE PROFESSION'S PERSPECTIVE

How can we account for the phenomenal growth of such a curriculum initiative at a time when almost all curriculum development activities were centrally directed and funded?

How did it all happen in the space of ten years?

The period of the award scheme emergence has witnessed some of the most radical changes in educational policy since state funding began in 1832. The partnership of the 1944 Act (between schools, LEAs and the government) has been replaced by the partnership of the 1990s between government prescribing the regulations, parents with the power to 'choose' and employers through sponsorship and membership of governing bodies. Control of curriculum matters has shifted away from schools, teachers and LEAs. Alongside this, professional autonomy has been dramatically challenged.

As many commentators acknowledge, there have been considerable gains arising from aspects of the 1988 Act and subsequent legislation – such as parental involvement, the notion of the 'entitlement curriculum' and financial autonomy. There have been losses too, some of which have been acutely felt by teachers. Expressive arts, personal and social education, beliefs in the value of the negotiated curriculum and teacher initiated innovation, curriculum breadth and such like have all taken a battering in recent years. Yet these things have always been valued by teachers (and indeed by most parents). It is with regard to some of these that the ASDAN Award Scheme has been able to make its mark.

Chapter 7 considered the views of teachers and lecturers in relation to curriculum development and professional autonomy. Their comments were also sought about the award scheme itself. All of them were running the award scheme in their respective establishments. Their observation and experiences are reflected here, and provide a professional perspective on the award scheme's success.

'It encourages independent learning, initiative and personal organizational skills'

The school's policy is to give ASDAN status by involving senior staff. It has helped to establish pastoral links with pupils and improve contact opportunities with parents. The school has benefited by having an option that promotes a working style which is nearer to GNVQ than many other subjects' styles. A balance of curriculum 'diet' is achieved for some pupils. The award scheme option period is also used as a 'lay by' experience for pupils to make sure their core subjects are up to date (negotiated of course!) Pupils like the opportunity of self-directed learning.

(Dewi Jones)

Excellent. It provides space to develop strategies appropriate to individual students. It encourages independent learning, initiative and personal organisational skills in ways in which the exam curriculum does not and cannot. The award scheme enables us to accredit many activities within the broader curriculum framework, such as work experience, community service, and group activities. Flexibility is its huge advantage.

(Jim Harnes)

Our recent Ofsted inspection noted that some pupils who had not hitherto achieved success were now doing so under the YAS. The value of the course is improved by its external moderation, and in the similarity to the format used for reporting evidence within NVQs, which many of our pupils will follow when they leave school.

(Geoffrey Osborn)

I regard the course as a breath of fresh air. It presents the opportunity to develop pupils self esteem in a relevant framework. All pupils seem very committed and enjoy working on real issues and I can already feel the confidence growing and personal skills developing. Other areas of the curriculum have noticed this also.

(Karen Jenkins)

The ASDAN awards have allowed me to work in an open learning situation, which, in an ideal world, is the way education should be delivered. Within the school it has enabled us to identify the full range of skills and talents which our youngsters possess, and the credit framework appears to act as a better incentive to record this information than Records of Achievement.

(Mike Creary)

I particularly favour the award scheme, as I feel it gives our students a sense of achievement when they gain their credits and certificates. They are able to achieve at their own pace and can see progression. The scheme is blessedly easy to administer and moderate, and the units of work fit easily within other schemes so that they can be run in conjunction.

(Neil Judges)

It's going back to a basic principle that all students can achieve in their own way. It offers a different approach that looks at what they can do, rather than confronting them with what they can't.

(Anon.)

It's an excellent all rounder; we would like to see further expansion both from ASDAN and in school. The method of accreditation is readily accessed by students and teaching staff. There are enormous benefits for pupils, such as confidence building, community awareness, and employment.

(Susan Downes)

The award scheme places learning within the students' grasp: they determine their progress; it is not imposed from outside. It is rigorous in that pupils must plan, decide on skills to be targeted, actively review, and take responsibility for their learning. It has become increasingly popular at my school and is oversubscribed.

(Anon.)

The scheme meets the needs of students and is recognised and welcomed by teachers. Enthusiasm at regional moderation never wanes. The knock on effect for students is immeasurable. YAS teachers tend to be totally committed to the ideals of the scheme, and are worth their weight in gold to students and the school.

(Hazel Saunders)

'It accredits the extra-curricular activities so necessary for UCAS/job applications'

This is the most encouraging thing I do in terms of helping me concentrate on the positive side of my pupils. The relaxed, student centred approach gives me all the advantages of FE in a school. It accredits achievement and gives an extra pat on the back to those who 'do' things for the school, and also enhances the perception of GNVQ. Students like the informal approach, and appreciate it's a good experience for university applications, reminding themselves how much they've done.

(Kath Grant)

We are now in our second year of using the Gold award in the sixth form as a student centred/driven PSE programme, instead of a general studies programme, because I wanted tutors to be involved. It's early days but ASDAN is here to stay as long as I am here.

(Bill Malty)

There are few areas of the curriculum where a teacher has as much opportunity to design his or her own curriculum, as is possible with YAS. The award scheme provides a link between academic subjects and

GNVQ core skills. It's important for students going into the workplace or on to higher education.

(Martin Fisher)

The Universities (Platinum level) award has provided us with a framework in which to develop and accredit core skills together with encouraging students to demonstrate a breadth of interest and involvement in the community. It has taken a while for students to really believe in the value of anything other than A levels. The UCAS form and interviews (and the press) have done much to convince them of the need to be more than just a good academic.

(Pam Taylor)

It's proving to be excellent for our students who are doing the Universities (Platinum level) award, alongside their A level studies. Students take more responsibility and it allows them to cover a variety of tasks, which breaks up their intensive subject studies. As teachers, we find out what makes the students tick in reviewing progress, which helps to build relationships. In attracting future students, the award scheme is a good marketing device, since current students talk about it to their peers.

(Anon.)

The scheme is student centred, flexible and with a breadth which allows it to encompass almost all types of programme for all types of students. It has helped my course team develop a more co-ordinated approach to each student's studies. GCSE projects can be assessed for the core skills elements. We use IT computer studies as a linchpin. In the future, it will be encouraged at level 3 for A level students, both as an opportunity for curriculum enrichment and to provide evidence of core skills.

(Linda Chance)

The Universities award accredits the extra curricular activities such as life saving and sign language skills and so on, which are so valuable for UCAS and job applications. It gives the students an additional purpose in relation to these activities, and helps them value themselves.

(D. Dace)

'A vehicle for delivery of core skills'

The award scheme offers a chance to develop learning experiences with a free conscience! Core skills require no justification and the awards are recognized by a growing range of impressive organizations.

(Ivan Prokaza)

As an accompaniment to GNVQ I feel ASDAN is a useful vehicle to support the core skills element without overburdening the student with inappropriate or irrelevant tasks. It also assists the tutors to know more about particular interests.

(Mark Read)

The award scheme is the most logical and common sense method of giving validity to the important/essential life skills that employers demand

(and many pupils possess, but which are not formally recognized). For the school it offers a structured system of presenting all the essentials, above and beyond (and even within) the exam syllabus. For the pupils it offers recognition of their qualities other than just academic success.

(J. Jones)

I have recently seen how important the award scheme is in terms of teaching or introducing core skills to students, especially when we aim for them to go on to post-16 courses.

(Becky Bedford)

The ASDAN framework offers superb flexibility to develop the interpersonal skills via an individualised programme. The students have enjoyed the challenges, particularly those that are IT based, and we are hoping to move forward and actually gain the NCVQ accreditation for the core skills.

(Lesley Harrison)

The ASDAN Award Scheme has enabled us to find a vehicle for delivery and awareness of core skills for all students in a 14–19 school. It has also allowed us to introduce a vocational framework for everyone, without the sheep/goats syndrome of GNVQs/A levels or GCSE/Foundation.

(John Edwards)

The ASDAN scheme, running through core skills, places a challenge on the student to integrate all their skills, knowledge and experience and reflect upon their learning. It offers teachers the chance to assist the student to explore new avenues of thought and discuss. The scheme enables students to identify their strengths, have some control over their own learning and is seen as relevant to their personal and social development.

(Frank Byle)

'It opens up opportunities for better relationships'

A PSE programme is being introduced to our school and I have decided to use the extra 70 minutes per week to run the youth awards across the sixth form. It is envisaged that the majority of the students will gain a Gold award. Benefits to staff: an opportunity to offer modules in which they have a personal interest, autonomy and a closer working relationship with some students. Benefits to students: choice, flexibility, responsibility for organization of own route through the system, national accreditation, confidence, autonomy and core skills highlighted and emphasized.

(J. Barron)

It is a brilliant way of accrediting students for the skills which they possess, outside of the academic world. It also enables the teacher to have a better understanding of individuals and their lives outside of school. It teaches them independence and prepares them for GNVQ courses.

(Julia Hollingworth)

As a teacher it is a valuable focus to talk to students about issues other than the taught curriculum. Therefore it opens up opportunities for better relationships. It has been a useful vehicle to accredit personal and social education (PSE) – i.e. what our students are doing already. It allows them to display their talents on a broader canvas and has encouraged them to try other things.

(Clive Baker)

It offers teachers opportunities for discussion with students on subjects not necessarily related to academic subjects, which enables them to find out more about the 'whole' student.

(Judy Miles)

'A brilliant addition to the curriculum'

It is essential now as a scheme in our school. It has enriched the curriculum. Other innovations have taken place as a result of the ASDAN example.

(Ray Banks)

It has provided the framework within which our year 10/11 pupils can begin to work towards their independence, whilst acquiring a nationally recognized qualification. The scheme has enabled cross-curricular activities to take place and pupil achievements in other areas of the curriculum to be recognized.

(Shelley Reddan)

ASDAN allows us to accredit 'enrichment activities', such as work experience, PE, expressive arts, and outside interests. It also allows us to accredit skill development across the curriculum (e.g. information handling), which benefits the students as they can direct their learning and record their achievements.

(Janet Pugh)

Potentially ASDAN schemes give teachers greater professional control to enrich the opportunities students have to work and learn. The accreditation framework enables students to take a more active role in their own education and an investment in the learning process.

(Gareth Lewis)

As a curriculum enrichment activity it is extremely useful. It gives status to the PSE programme and rewards pupils for their work in this area. It helps students focus on the development of their action planning and core skills.

(Sue-Anne Jenkins)

It verifies and gives certification for things already being done by our students. It has also helped us to further develop our complementary studies programme in main school and our foundation programme in the sixth form.

(John Nunn)

It gives accreditation and a framework for favourite projects and topics not strictly covered by the national curriculum, and provides a focus for the Key Stage 4 (KS4) curriculum. There is greater motivation in KS4 as a result, because it gives pupils a sense of self-esteem (e.g. from interim certificates for modules) and self-direction.

(Wendy Chandler)

ASDAN has provided a much needed core study programme in years 10, 11 and 12. It fits into our vocational programme very well and has helped to motivate our students.

(S. Bull)

It has offered a form of accreditation for something many of us were already doing with our students.

(Susan Whitehead)

We have found that the ASDAN framework has allowed us to develop a full-time pastoral curriculum which is tailor made for our students. It also teaches them that being a student is not just about passing exams, but is also about development of the whole person, both academically and socially.

(Lesley Harrison)

A brilliant addition to the curriculum. I see it as a way of accrediting future courses such as personal and social education, religious education and health education.

(Stefka Makorkij)

'The Award Scheme keeps me sane'

For me as a teacher (and my colleagues teaching on the course) we value the input we can make to provide a relevant and interesting programme of work. The school has benefited enormously as we have taken the scheme into the community – helping the local church for example – and we have received praiseworthy publicity in the press.

(Gwyn Evans)

ASDAN enables teachers who value the pupil centred approach, the modular approach, and the process models of curriculum planning to develop as professionals, and facilitate innovation and creativity in an otherwise stale, potentially inhibiting curriculum.

(Ray Banks)

The accreditation framework is a crucial development. The ASDAN approach to verification compared to awarding bodies like City and Guilds and BTEC is much more teacher led.

(K. Truman)

I feel that the award scheme is the one glimmer of hope in a dark turgid sea of political manipulation. It allows me to put in place essential curriculum development work which still has relevance.

(Lesley Preece)

The Youth Award Scheme has developed extremely well and all of the colleagues I come into contact with, across Nottinghamshire, who are involved with it are committed to the scheme, thus helping its profile as a professionally run/taught alternative to GNVQs and GCSEs.

(Sandra Small)

Brilliant for me professionally. It offered a springboard that gave me the confidence to get involved in other skill based courses. It's a viable and credible way for students to be given recognition for their qualities and skills, which has knock on effects in other lessons.

(Hazel Saunders)

Excellent. It enables easy access to a good cross-curricular programme, which develops students and the basic skills required to follow a career.

(J. Wrathall)

As a teacher it's been an enjoyable rewarding experience, although I am now returning to my specialism, English. It was commented on very positively by Ofsted, who saw it as of benefit to the social and moral welfare of students.

(Erica Moores)

The Award Scheme keeps me sane! Whilst being a nationally recognized scheme, it gives teachers the freedom and opportunity to try out innovative ideas and gives pupils a different experience that they really value. It is probably the most adult experience that our youngsters have, and it is very manageable.

(Graham Wright)

I've been pleased with the scheme. It does most of what has already been going on in PSE with the added advantage of the outcomes and skills being recognized.

(C. Morrish)

ASDAN works because it was developed by teachers who have daily contact with real students. It has managed to please students, staff, senior management, and the FEFC. I sometimes wonder if line-management structures are responsible for de-professionalism as it is now very difficult to get any direct communication with people who make decisions. Perhaps horizontal, rather than vertical, structures would be more effective. Additionally, the trend for targets set by government and quangos, to be reached in order to get funding, does not allow staff or students to make the most of their time in education. We are having to be obsessed with the achievement of vocational qualifications or Schedule 2 programmes, when the students' real needs may be to do with personal/social/life skills before moving on. The only awarding body to tackle this seems to be ASDAN, providing a relevant, realistic curriculum and accreditation.

(Linda Chance)

As a teacher-led curriculum development, ASDAN is remarkable and exciting for students.

(Maureen Wilsdon)

'For special school teachers it is a godsend'

For the teacher there is some flexibility which can be used to follow pupils' interests and abilities. Students are achieving and are motivated. It is a useful programme which meets the needs of the special needs group (14–16). Students enjoy the work. They have to take responsibility for their own learning, and can use their work in their Record of Achievement for college/jobs at 16 plus.

(Bridget Jebb)

Absolutely fabulous. We operate Bronze with our moderate learning difficulty (MLD) students. It's wonderful to have an award that our pupils (in general) can achieve. It's easy to operate, attractive to use and easy to assess. For years special schools have spent a lot of time, energy and money on things to help our pupils become more independent and socially acceptable. There have been few ways to recognize this all in one, easy to operate system, with the results kept in one, easy to read, booklet. It means progression really happens – we start Bronze here and it's continued at college into Silver. It's a good motivator; students know that everything they do can be assessed and it makes learning relevant to life.

(Kiri Garbut)

It is the hardest subject I 'teach' (support). It is an external accreditation that our students can realistically aspire to. Ask the pupils their views – the best subject all week. They are enthusiastic and realistic. By constantly reviewing their work with them on a 1:1 basis you begin to get the students self-evaluating their work, and some of them extending themselves beyond all your hopes.

(Heather Wallace)

It has been regularly mentioned by Ofsted and HMI who seem to hold it in high regard. It has been a focus to empower children who traditionally have little control over their learning. It gives structure to action planning, success against criteria that they can achieve, and it offers a progression route to college.

(Elizabeth Downie)

For special school teachers it is a godsend! The accreditation of these achievements and the collection of evidence in pupil portfolios offers a very comprehensive method of planning, doing and evaluation – it also gives teachers back the opportunity to be involved in all three steps and properly accredit work the pupils do.

(Peggy Walpole)

The Youth Award Scheme has been a godsend to our post 16 students. As a school for severe learning difficulty (SLD) pupils aged 2–19, it has long been acknowledged that the 14–19-year group need a challenging scheme of work in the life skills area. YAS fills this bill. Although we are only still piloting the scheme, its evident ultimate success is already apparent. Students particularly like the ownership of the handbooks.

(Christine Harrison)

I have sought appropriate accreditation for over five years for MLD students. When introduced to YAS I was immediately impressed and excited to find such cross-curricular accreditation, which has helped to structure the delivery of the curriculum. It has also helped to form links with specialist teachers. It aids transition by accrediting 'non-exam' students' prior learning, helping them plan their work via challenge planner, and identifying their core skills. Useful networks have been established.

(Elaine Poppleton)

THE ALCHEMIST'S SKILL

From analysis of the above comments and those of other practitioners involved with the scheme it is clear that there are various interlinked factors that explain the success of the ASDAN Award Scheme. Its capacity to meet the needs of individual students and teachers, while addressing institutional concerns and priorities, is clearly very significant.

Through the various sets of student workbooks, targeted at different levels, it offers an 'off the shelf' curriculum enrichment package, which can embrace or extend what classroom teachers are doing already. Work experience, health education, personal and social education, the expressive arts, sporting activities and such like are all included. The remodelling of the scheme over the years in response to identified need has taken place, while preserving the essential ingredients of success. New programmes to cater for 'special needs', such as *Towards Independence* and *Workright*, have been developed alongside the introduction of a Platinum/Universities award which has been welcomed by UCAS in relation to student applications to university.

The Platinum Award really does complement the studies of sixth form students. What we particularly notice here is that it increases the confidence of the students, greatly improves their self image, and gives credit for activities that are beyond the ordinary curriculum and which play an important part in their personal and social development.

(Sister Brigid Halligan, Head of St Mary's
RC High School, Liverpool)[1]

This is as true for Key Stage 4 as it is for the post-16 phase. Areas of experience that have been squeezed or marginalized because of National Curriculum requirements can be nurtured and enhanced by the accreditation offered by ASDAN. And the accreditation itself is now worth something in the market place. The acknowledgement of its value by higher education providers and employers' organizations, in response to the mention of the Gold and Platinum (now called Universities) levels in the UCAS Guide to Applicants has enhanced its image for those aspiring to university entrance (UCAS 1996). Seventeen- and eighteen-year-old students recognize that admission tutors are looking for a more extensive profile of achievement than that provided simply by A level or GNVQ points.

With the Platinum Award it goes down and it's recorded, so not only have you got something to look back on, but you can also take these achievements to prospective employers, universities and other education establishments. It's really beneficial.

(Matthew Brown, aged 17, Liverpool)

The Platinum Award is very good for UCAS applications. It shows that you can be committed to other things, that you can take responsibility, and that you've got a lot more going for you. I feel I've gained a lot of time management skills and a lot of confidence. I'm more able to communicate. I'll give anything a go.

(Ann Withall, aged 18, Ilfracombe)

The emphasis on 'core skills' (and now 'key skills' following the 1996 Dearing Report) means that those programmes that offer a template for both demonstrating and accrediting these are becoming increasingly attractive. The allocation of a points tariff for 'key/core skills' by UCAS will enhance the value of ASDAN's higher level awards yet further. Indeed, the Dearing Review drew attention to the potential of the ASDAN award scheme for recognizing a wider range of achievement, including 'those with exceptional ability' (DfEE 1996). This facility to 'kitemark' its awards with the NCVQ logo, for specific core/key skill accreditation at levels 1–3, made a big difference for ASDAN. Students engaged on A level or GNVQ courses can look to the ASDAN Universities Award for a means to demonstrate their competence in the personal skill area.

I'm doing four A levels – history, French and English, and I'll be starting general studies next year. I'm hoping to go on to university to study law and eventually to be a family law solicitor. I don't think there's anything else apart from the Award Scheme that helps us to work with people, to communicate and stuff like that.

(Emma Harris, aged 17, Bromsgrove)

My plans for the future are to go into medicine, especially surgery. There's a lot of competition out there for medicine, so having something like the Platinum Award gives you that little bit extra. It shows that you can do a lot more than just pass examinations.

(Samah Aliman, aged 17, Liverpool)

There is a strong correlation between student achievement in university and certain personal skills – the ability to wean themselves from dependence upon teachers, the ability to set their own agenda and to plan their own work, to develop study skills, to work in groups, to embark with courage on projects which need initiative and so on. In other words, success academically depends on certain personal and social skills – the core skills which are represented in the ASDAN Award Scheme.

(Richard Pring, Professor of Educational Studies
at Oxford University)

Some are wary of the recent emphasis on skills, particularly where the emphasis is on the demonstration of competence rather than the provision of evidence of knowledge and understanding (Jonathan 1983; Hodkinson 1992; Hyland 1994). This was part of Alan Smithers's concern when he described GNVQs as a 'disaster of epic proportions' (Smithers 1993), echoing a view expressed a decade earlier by the one quango that still represented the perspectives of the profession.

> A skill is more than knowing, and more than knowing how. It is action too. A skill involves the application of knowledge to achieve some anticipated outcome. It needs the capacity and the will to act, as well as knowledge.
>
> (Schools Council 1981)

The ASDAN Award Scheme provides just this opportunity to demonstrate application of knowledge in pursuit of activities that are seen as inherently worthwhile (and enjoyable) by the majority of students – so that the accreditation of key skills is part of a much broader process for students and staff. The 'enjoyment' aspect is clearly important too.

> I definitely recommend the scheme. It's good fun. I'm learning a new computer language, doing special effects stage lighting for the school play, and work experience for a theatre company called Stage Electrics. It allows you to do what you want to do and at the end it gives you a qualification which can be useful in later life, especially when you're trying to get into university.
>
> (Chris Tomlinson, aged 16, Bristol)

> I've very much enjoyed doing the Platinum Award, particularly working with other people – the Scouts and the basketball team, for example. It has helped me see what I want to do when I leave school. Originally I thought I wanted to be a teacher, but hopefully I'll go on to be a basketball coach instead.
>
> (Alex Smith, aged 17, Leominster)

Students find the challenges accessible and relevant. Very often they discover that they can obtain accreditation for things they have wanted to do anyway – passing their driving test, travelling on an 'inter-rail' ticket across Europe, running a fund raising charity event, organizing a period of work experience, improving their IT skills and so on. Motivation is enhanced at all levels. For teachers the scheme offers the opportunity to be involved once again in curriculum design and implementation, and in the follow through process of accreditation. The Mode 3 style consortium and moderation approach touches a chord about 'professional judgement' with older teachers, and stimulates the enthusiasm of younger staff.

It may be this dimension that is actually the most important. It harks back to the discussion in Chapter 4 on the significance of the affective domain: 'that most of us acquire knowledge and skills in a manner that is more influenced by the context in which we learn or by our feelings at the time', and that 'learning is a matter of challenges to and reformulation of personal theories and personal constructs, and that the role of the teacher is to lubricate these processes' (page 46).

What the teachers and lecturers have referred to in the comments above is magic at work. It is what Tim Brighouse (1994) encapsulated in his description of the 'teacher's extra-ordinary skill as an alchemist to the mind in transforming mental slavery to freedom.' The ASDAN Award Scheme provides the template for such magicians.

NOTE

1 Sister Brigid Halligan, Matthew Brown, Ann Withall, Emma Harris, Samah Aliman, Chris Tomlinson, Alex Smith and Professor Richard Pring were interviewed for *The Universities Award*, a video produced by Paul Gilbert for ASDAN in February 1996. This video is available from ASDAN (telephone: 0117 923 9843).

Conclusion

In discussions about ways forward in relation to the 14–19 curriculum, it is often asserted that 'the devil is in the detail'. I'm not so sure.

It seems to me one of the problems we are confronting is that the focus has been on the detail of the map at the expense of the territory itself – examining the daubs and dashes of the picture instead of studying the framework of the canvas.

What shines through these pages, particularly in the comments from teachers and lecturers, is a professional commitment to working with young people and a competence to do this effectively. They are quite able to work out the detail. The whole history of curriculum development is rich in examples of teachers as innovators. If the profession is trusted to manage the process of curriculum design and implementation, it is clear that schools can deliver the goods.

What is less clear is the broader canvas.

We have a divided and divisive system in the UK. One-third of our young people 'succeed' in acquiring sufficient 'points' to merit entrance to university, one-third achieve some limited success, often regarded as second best because of its vocational orientation, and one-third drop out at the earliest opportunity. The system only serves a minority of people very well indeed, and we need to ask some searching questions about why this is.

In addition, most debate about curriculum issues focuses on course design and content for the statutory sector, allowing the independent sector to select its response. It is as if only maintained schools and colleges need to be regulated, even though (or perhaps because?) the percentage of young people gaining university places from independent schools is proportionally higher than that from state schools.

Any debate about the ends (and means) of education can only make sense in the context of a consideration of the *whole* range of provision in the UK and the purposes that each part serves. Piecemeal analysis (such as that which only focuses on the maintained and less affluent sector) and knee jerk responses (such as those that follow any media reportage of 'success stories' in another country) will not help us to evolve a national framework. In a context where traditional expectations of employment opportunities no longer apply, where the social and community fabrics in some parts of the United Kingdom appear to be stretched to breaking point and where inequalities of all kinds (such as wealth and health) are reliably reported to be increasing, there needs to be a more considered debate about where we are heading, and the role of education in this broader vision.

It comes back to values, of course, and to some of the questions raised in Chapter 3.

What are we trying to achieve through our system of formal education? What do we want from the many billions of pounds that are spent on the public sector and the lesser billions spent on the private sector? What qualities do we want to develop and celebrate in young people? What knowledge, skills and competences are going to be most useful for them and for the country in the next century?

What sort of society do we actually want?

Answers to that question will not come easily. But they will only come if the debate is informed and informative, and if the views of all the partners in the educational process are taken seriously.

It is hoped that this book can contribute to such a debate.

appendix _____

Respondents to questionnaire survey

Linda Abbey, Nottinghamshire; Clive Baker, Cornwall; Tony Ballard, Devon; John Bament, Somerset; Lindsay Banks, Gwynedd; Ray Banks, Hertfordshire; J. Barron, Dorset; Val Bates, Nottinghamshire; A. Beaumont, Hertfordshire; Becky Bedford, Cambridge; Howard Bell, Cleveland; Jayne Bennett, Durham; Sharon Bennett, Dorset; Christina Berry, Kent; Ian Booth, Cumbria; H. Bowles, Hampshire; Mary Brennan, Dorset; Sue Brooks, Kent; Richard Brown, Norfolk; Sue Brown; M. Bryan, Tyne and Wear; S. Bull, Essex; Mike Bullen, Bristol; Nicholas Bush, Nottinghamshire; A. Butler, Surrey; Frank Byle, Hertfordshire; Mike Carver, Surrey; Colin Chamberlain, Kent; Linda Chance, Gloucestershire; Sheila Chennels, West Midlands; Wendy Chandler, Dorset; Jacalin Chawner, Essex; Mike Church, Lincoln; Philippa Clark, Dorset; Debbie Clayfield, Avon; Anne Clifford, Dorset; P. Collins, Tyne and Wear; Phil Courage, Wiltshire; Mike Creary, West Yorkshire; Anne Crease, Devon; Roger Cupit; Lynne Cutts, Suffolk; D. Dace, Cambridgeshire; Sally Davies, Essex; Catherine Devine, Merseyside; Elizabeth Downie, South Yorkshire; Susan Downes, North Yorkshire; Christie Drakeley, Cornwall; Paddy Ducey, South Yorkshire; A. Dunn, Staffordshire; P. Dyson, Hertfordshire; B. Earl, Cumbria; Christine Edwards, East Sussex; John Edwards, Leicestershire; E. Evans, Staffordshire; Gwyn Evans, Middlesex; Martin Fisher, Nottinghamshire; Jan Foster, Surrey; Julie Friel, Greater Manchester; Paul Fursland, Gwent; Kiri Garbit, Wiltshire; Dilys Garnett, Greater Manchester; Carole Gibbs, Worcestershire; John Goldring, Harrogate; Angela Gooseman, Humberside; Kath Grant, Northumberland; Dr Richard Gurnham, Lincolnshire; Derek Hadden, Bristol; Paul Hammond, West Yorkshire; Janet Harden, Avon; Jim Harmes, Nottinghamshire; Christine Harrison, South Yorkshire; Lesley Harrison, Cambridgeshire; Judith Harwood, North Humberside; Steve Heigham, Somerset; Beryl Henshaw, Oxfordshire; Che Hill, Cambridge; Julia Hollingworth, Greater London; A. Hoodless, West Yorkshire; Austin Howard, London; Keith Hutt, Hertfordshire; David Ibbotson, Oxfordshire; Bridget Jebb, Northamptonshire; Karen Jenkins, Middlesex; Sue-Anne Jenkins, Kent; Dewi Jones, Berkshire; J. Jones; Neil Judges, Kent; Lyn Kite, Lincolnshire; Jennie Kitteringham, London; Sheila Knight; F. Langford; Paul Lawrence, Tyne and Wear; Veronica Lawrence, Warwickshire; Graham Legg, Oxfordshire; Myra Levine, Humberside; David Lewis, Hertfordshire; Gareth Lewis, Oxfordshire; Bette Liddell, Northern Ireland; Pat Lockett, Nottinghamshire; Elaine Lowe, Lancashire; Linda McGinn, Devon; Ian McLachlan, Cornwall; Stefka Makorkij, Cambridgeshire; Bill Malty, West Sussex; J. Marsh, Essex; Mary Marsh, Kent; Philip Maud,

Leeds; Judy Miles, Dorset; D. Millard, Marlborough; Fiona Miller, Leeds; Erica Moores, West Yorkshire; C. Morrish, Essex; Elaine Nightingale, Essex; Gill Noel, Portsmouth; John Nunn, Norfolk; Adele O'Connor, Gloucester; Dil Owen, Cambridge; Gary Owens, Mid Glamorgan; Liz Parham, Oxfordshire; Liz Parker, Oxfordshire; Des Pejko, Nottinghamshire; Mike Pendry, Hertfordshire; Mo Pepper, Staffordshire; Jane Pereira, South Glamorgan; Jan Perry, Lincolnshire; Yvonne Pickersgill, Devon; Vicki Ponsford, Gloucestershire; Elaine Poppleton, South Yorkshire; Lesley Preece, East Sussex; Ivan Prokaza, Nottinghamshire; S. Pruss; Geraint Pugh, London; Janet Pugh, London; Penelope Rea, Suffolk; Mark Read, Essex; Shelley Reddan, Hampshire; Anna Roberts, Gwynedd; Madeleine Salter-Vaughan, Worcestershire; E. Sanders, Leicestershire; Hazel Saunders, Avon; Chris Savory, East Sussex; Janet Schofield, Bedfordshire; Tessa Seaman, Norfolk; Jean Shaw, Liverpool; C. Short, West Yorkshire; Jane Shorter, Kent; Dave Simmons, Dorset; Pete Sinfield, Cambridgeshire; Sandra Small, Nottinghamshire; Lilian Smart, Middlesex; N. Smith, East Sussex; Linette Springer; Philip Storer, Staffordshire; Brett Storry, Cheshire; Susan Summers, Lincolnshire; Pam Taylor, Worcestershire; R. Tipper, Staffordshire; Liz Towers, Essex; Chris Traxson, Birmingham; K. Truman, Nottinghamshire; Margaret Tucker, Avon; Colin Twigg, Essex; Philippa Wadsworth, Norfolk; M. Walker, Lincolnshire; Heather Wallace, Surrey; Peggy Walpole, London; Sue Weston, London; Pete Whalen, Leicester; Susan Whitehead, Hereford; Colin Whittaker, Somerset; Martin Wilcox, Essex; G. Wild, Greater Manchester; Jane Williams, Essex; Maureen Wilsdon, Newcastle upon Tyne; Eric Winstone, Cambridgeshire; Diane Wraight, Dorset; J. Wrathall, Surrey; Graham Wright, West Yorkshire.

Bibliography

Abbott, J. (1993) *Education 2000*. Letchworth: Education 2000.

Adams, G., Hanza, M., Day, D., Spiller, P., Dourneen, J., Gallie, P., Lawton, B., Taylor, M., Benson, D., Fettes, T., Hobbs, B., Everett Rimmer, S., Hawkes, V., Brown, T., Wightman, P., Plant, S. and White, R. (1987) *The Youth Award Scheme Staff Handbook*. Bristol: Bristol Polytechnic.

Adamson, J. (1964) *English Education 1789–1902*. Cambridge: Cambridge University Press.

AEC (1989) *The Hobart Declaration*. Melbourne: Australian Education Council.

Ahier, J. and Flude, M. (eds) (1983) *Contemporary Education Policy*. London: Croom Helm.

Andresen, A. (1992) *The Folkehojskole Today*. Copenhagen: Folkehojskole Association.

Bach, P. and Christensen, C. (1992) From despair to optimism: the success story of Danish education, *RSA Journal*, June, 443–51.

Bailey, C. (1984) *Beyond the Present and the Particular*. London: Routledge & Kegan Paul.

Baker, K. (1993) *The Turbulent Years: My Life in Politics*. London: Faber & Faber.

Balboni, P. (1993) Language awareness in the national curriculum for language education in Italy, *Language Awareness*, 2 (4).

Baldwin, J. and Wells, H. (1979–1984) *Active Tutorial Work Volumes 1–6*. London: Blackthorns.

Ball, C. (1991) *Learning Pays: the Role of Post-compulsory Education and Training*. London: Royal Society of Arts.

Ball, C. (1993) *Start Right*. London: RSA.

Barber, M. (1996) Steady funding growth is key to success, *Times Educational Supplement*, 10 May.

Barnett, C. (1986) *The Audit of War*. London: Macmillan.

BBC (1983) *Manpower Services Commission and the School*. London: BBC Publications.

BBC (1996) Hard lesson, *Panorama* documentary, 3 June 1996.

Bell, B. (1988) A different kind of democracy, *Times Educational Supplement*, 22 January.

Bennett, N. (1976) *Teaching Styles and Pupil Progress*. Wells: Open Books.

Berg, G. (1992) Changes in the steering of Swedish schools, *Journal of Curriculum Studies*, 24 (4), 327–44.

Bierhoff, H. (1996) *Laying the Foundations of Numeracy*. London: NIESR.

Bjerg, J. (1991) Reflections on Danish comprehensive education 1903–1990, *European Journal of Education*, 22 (2), 132–41.

Blagg, N. (1989) Thinking as a skill, *Education*, 174 (1), 11–12.

Blagg, N. (1991) *Can We Teach Intelligence? A Comprehensive Evaluation of Feuerstein's Instrumental Enrichment Program*. Hillsdale, NJ. Laurence Erlbaum.

Bodey, D.W. (1985) The management implications of APPIL, *Physics Education*, 2 (6), 298–304.

Bourdieu, P. (1974) The school as a conservative force: scholatic and cultural inequalities, in J. Eggleston (ed.) *Contemporary Research in the Sociology of Education*. London: Methuen.

Brighouse, T. (1994) The magicians of the inner city, *Times Educational Supplement*, 22 April, 29–30.

Brighouse, T. (1996) 2001 uses of a new millennium, *Times Educational Supplement*, 19 July.

Brockington, D. and White, R. (1986) *Organising a Negotiated Curriculum*. Bristol: Youth Education Service.

Bronowski, J. (1973) *The Ascent of Man*. London: BBC Publications.

Bruner, J. (1960) *The Process of Education*. Cambridge, MA: Harvard University Press.

Bruner, J. (1966) *Towards a Theory of Instruction*. Cambridge, MA: Harvard University Press.

Bruner, J. (1986) *Actual Minds, Possible Worlds*. Cambridge, MA: Harvard University Press.

Burstall, E. (1996) Blunkett's new comprehensive ideal, *Times Educational Supplement*, 1 March, 4.

Button, L. (1984) *Group Tutoring for the Form Teacher: Volumes 1 and 2*. London: Hodder & Stoughton.

Callaghan, J. (1976) Towards a National Debate, speech at Ruskin College, Oxford, reported in *Education*, 22 October.

Callaghan, J. (1987) *Time and Chance*. Glasgow: Collins.

Campbell, B., Lazonby, J., Millar, R., Nicolson, P., Ramsden, J. and Waddington, D. (1994) Science: the Salters' approach – a case study of the process of large scale curriculum development, *Science Education*, 78 (5), 415–47.

Carmichael, L. (chair) (1992) *The Australian Vocational Certificate Training System*. Report to AEC and MOVEET, Canberra.

Carter, D. (1993) Structural change and curriculum reform in an Australian education system, *International Journal of Educational Reform*, 2 (1).

CBI (1988) *Towards a Skills Revolution*. London: CBI.

CBI (1993) *A Credit to Your Career*. London: CBI.

Charter, D. (1995) 15,000 bad teachers should be sacked, *Times*, 3 November, 1.

Clatworthy, N. and Galbraith, P. (1991) Mathematics modelling in senior school mathematics: implementing an innovation, *Teaching Mathematics and its Applications*, 10 (1).

Clough, N. and Menter, I. (1995) Some Lessons from Latvia, *European Journal of Intercultural Studies*, 6 (2): 3–11.

Cox, B. (1992) *Cox on Cox: an English Curriculum for the 1990s*. London: Hodder & Stoughton.

Cox, B. and Dyson, A. (eds) (1969) *Fight for Education: a Black Paper* and *Black Paper Two*. London: Critical Society Quarterly.

Cranford, H. (1996) UK takes a lowly rank in spending league, *Times Educational Supplement*, 17 May, 14.

Crombie White, R., Pring, R. and Brockington, D. (1995) *14–19 Education and Training: Implementing a Unified System of Learning*. London: Royal Society of Arts.

Dale, R. *et al.* (1990) *The TVEI Story: Policy, Practice and Preparation for the Workforce*. Milton Keynes: Open University Press.

Dalton, T. (1988) *The Challenge of Curriculum Innovation: a Study of Ideology and Practice.* Lewes: Falmer Press.

Danish Ministry of Education (1976) *The Act of the Folkeskole.* Copenhagen.

Danish Ministry of Education and Research (1992) *Education in Denmark.* Copenhagen.

Dearing Report (1994) *The National Curriculum and its Assessment.* London: SCAA.

Department of Employment (1994) *Competitiveness: Helping Business to Win.* London: HMSO.

DES (1977) *Education in Schools: a Consultative Document.* London: HMSO.

DES (1979) *Local Authority Arrangements for the School Curriculum.* London: HMSO.

DES (1980) *A Framework for the School Curriculum.* London: HMSO.

DES (1981) *The School Curriculum.* London: HMSO.

DES (1982) *The Lower Attaining Pupils Programme (LAPP).* London: HMSO.

DES (1984) *Records of Achievement: a Statement of Policy.* London: HMSO.

DES (1985) *Better Schools.* London: HMSO.

DES (1991) *Education and Training for the 21st Century.* London: HMSO.

DfE (1992) *Choice and Diversity.* London: HMSO.

DfE (1995) *Circular 3/95: Statutory Approval of Qualifications under Section 5 of Education Reform Act 1988.* London: DFE Publications.

DfEE (1996) *Report on the Review of Qualifications for 16 to 19 Year Olds* (known as the Dearing Post-16 Review). London: HMSO.

Dewey, J. (1916) *Democracy and Education.* New York: Free Press.

Dickens, C. (1852) *Hard Times.* Harmondsworth: Penguin (1995 edn).

Donaldson, M. (1993) *Human Minds.* Harmondsworth: Penguin.

Donoughue, B. (1987) *Prime Minister: the Conduct of Policy under Harold Wilson and James Callaghan.* London: Jonathan Cape.

Edwards, T., Fitz, J., Whitty, G. (1989) *State and Private Education: an evaluation of the Assisted Places Scheme.* Lewes: Falmer Press.

Eggleston, J. (1977) *The Sociology of the School Curriculum.* London: Routledge & Kegan Paul.

Eggleston, J. (1980) School Based Curriculum Development in Britain. London: Routledge & Kegan Paul.

Eilerman, R. and Stanley, M. (1994) A collaborative model to help beginning teachers prepare materials for their first years of teaching, *Teaching and Change,* 2 (1).

Eisner, E. (1991) Should America have a national curriculum?, *Educational Leadership,* October.

Eisner, E. (1993) Invitational conference on the hidden consequences of a national curriculum, *Educational Researcher,* October.

Eliot, J. (1996) The renewal of the education system in Slovakia: reflections on two Western European funded initiatives, in D. James (ed.) *The Redland Papers.* Bristol: UWE Faculty of Education.

Ellis, T., McWhirter, J., McColgan, D. and Haddow, B. (1976) *William Tyndale: the Teachers' Story.* London: Writers and Readers Publishing Co-operative.

Engineering Council (1993) *A Review of Engineering Formation.* London: Engineering Council.

Eurostat (1991) *A Social Portrait of Europe.* Brussels: Directorate for Social and Regional Statistics.

Eurydice (1991) *Education and Initial Training Systems in the Member States of the European Community.* Brussels.

Finegold, D., Keep, E., Milliband, D., Raffe, D. and Spours, K. (1990) *A British Baccalaureate.* London: The Institute for Public Policy Research.

Finn, B. (chair) (1991) *Young People's Participation in Post-compulsory Education and Training.* Report of the AEC Review committee. AGPS: Canberra.

Fletcher, B. (1983) The Exeter Award Scheme, *Journal of the National Organisation for Initiatives in Social Education*, 2 (2), 9.

Fowler, W. (1988) *Towards the National Curriculum: Discussion and Control in the English Educational System 1965–1988*. London: Kogan Page.

Fromm, E. (1956) *The Sane Society*. London: Allen & Unwin.

Fullick, P. (1992) Addressing science and technology issues in the United Kingdom: the SATIS project, *Theory into Practice*, 31 (1).

Further Education Unit (1995) *A Framework for Credit*. London: FEU.

Gardner, H. (1993) *Multiple Intelligence: the Theory in Practice*. New York: Basic Books.

Ginsberg, H. and Opper, S. (1969) *Piaget's Theory of Intellectual Development*. New York: Prentice Hall.

Gleeson, D. *et al.* (1988) *TVEI and Secondary Education*. Milton Keynes: Open University Press.

Gleeson, D. and McClean, M. (1994) Whatever happened to TVEI? TVEI, curriculum and schooling, *Journal of Education Policy*, 9 (3), 233–44.

Goodlad, J. (1984) *A Place Called School*. New York: McGraw-Hill.

Granada TV (1981) *Chalkface*.

Gretton, J. and Jackson, M. (1976) *William Tyndale: Collapse of a School – or a System?* London: Allen & Unwin.

Gronsved, W. (1986) *School–Home Co-operation in the Danish Folkeskole*. Paris: OECD.

Hackett, G. (1996) Labour in fresh row over selection, *Times Educational Supplement*, 8 March, 4.

Halsall, R. and Cockett, M. (eds) (1996) *Education and Training 14–19: Chaos or Coherence?* London: Fulton Press.

Halstead, M. (1986) Woven into the existing curriculum: a case study of peace education at Carlton-Bolling School, *Cambridge Journal of Education*, 17 (1), 41–9.

Hargreaves, A. *et al.* (1995) Teachers – the forgotten heroes, *Times Educational Supplement*, 31 March, supplement.

Hargreaves, D. (1980) Three new Rs, *Times Educational Supplement*, 10 October, 25.

Harlen, W. (1973) Science 5–13 project, in *Evaluation in Curriculum Development: Twelve Case Studies*. London, Macmillan.

Harrison, C. (1996) Take a leaf out of the Scots' book, *Times Educational Supplement*, 17 May, 10.

Haviland, J. (ed.) (1988) *Take care, Mr. Baker! A selection from the Advice on the Government's Education Reform Bill which the Secretary of State Invited but Decided not to Publish*. London: Fourth Estate.

HMI (1977a) *Ten Good Schools*. London: HMSO.

HMI (1977b) *Curriculum 11–16*. London: HMSO.

HMI (1978) *Mixed Ability Work in the Comprehensive School*. London: HMSO.

HMI (1979) *Aspects of Secondary Education*. London: HMSO.

HMI (1980) *A View of the Curriculum*. London: HMSO.

HMI/DES (1982) *Teacher Training and Preparation for Working Life*. London: HMSO.

HMI (1985) *Better Schools*. London: HMSO.

Heys, G. (1996) Outraged by the Chief Inspector (letter), *Times Educational Supplement*, 1 March.

Hillgate Group (1987) *The Reform of British Education: from Principles to Practice*. London: The Hillgate Group.

Hirsch, E. (1987) *Cultural Literacy: What Every American Needs to Know*. Boston: Houghton & Mifflin.

Hodges, L. (1996) Defenders rally round the old flag, *Times Educational Supplement*, 8 March, 10.

Hodkinson, P. (1992) Alternative models of competence in vocational education and training, *Journal of Further and Higher Education*, 16 (2), 30–9.

Hoeg, P. (1994) *Miss Smilla's Feeling for Snow*. London: Flamingo.

Hofkins, D. (1996a) Making sense of the results, *Times Educational Supplement*, 2 February, 13.

Hofkins, D. (1996b) Sixties were heady not barmy, *Times Educational Supplement*, 16 February, 4.

Hofkins, D. and Hackett, G. (1996) Tests revive boycott fear, *Times Educational Supplement*, 9 February, 1.

HTV (1980) Tackling truancy news report, 2 December.

Hughes, P. (1992) Curriculum implementation: a national and a personal issue, *Educational Research and Perspectives*, 19 (1).

Hughes, P. (1994) Diversification of secondary education, in OECD Report on Conference *Issues in Education in Asia and the Pacific*. Paris: OECD.

Hutchinson, B. (1991) Active tutorial work, discussion and educational research, *British Educational Research Journal*, 17 (1).

Hutton, W. (1996) *The State We Are In*. London: Vintage Books.

Hyland, T. (1994) *Competence, Education and NVQs*. London: Cassell.

Institute for Public Policy Research (1993) *Education: a Different Vision. An Alternative White Paper*. London: IPPR.

Jonathan, R. (1983) The Manpower Services model of education, *Cambridge Journal of Education*, 13 (2), 9.

Jones, W. (1970) *Denmark*. London: Ernest Benn.

Kempton, T. and Allsop, T. (1985) Science in society – a local development study, *School Science Review*, 239.

Kirk, G. (1989) The growth of central influence on the curriculum, in B. Cosin *et al.* (eds) *School, Work and Equality*. Milton Keynes: Open University Press.

Kliebard, H. (1986) *The Struggle for the American Curriculum 1893–1958*. Boston: Routledge & Kegan Paul.

Koestler, A. (1970) *The Act of Creation*. London: Pan Books.

Kolb, D. (1984) *Experiential Learning: Experience as the Source of Learning*. Englewood Cliffs, NJ: Prentice Hall.

Kramer, L. (1991) Correct in general but short on specifics, *The Australian*.

Labour Party (1995) *Excellence for Everyone*. London: Labour Party.

Labour Party (1996) *Aiming Higher*. London: Labour Party.

Lawson, J. and Silver, H. (1973) *A Social History of Education in England*. London: Methuen.

Lawton, D. (1984) The tightening grip: Central control of the school curriculum, *Bedford Way Papers 21*. London: University of London Institute of Education.

Lawton, D. (1989) *Education, Culture and the National Curriculum*. London: Hodder & Stoughton.

Lawton, D. (1992) *Education and Politics in the 1990s: Conflict or Consensus?* London: Falmer Press.

Lawton, D. (1993) Curriculum policy development since the Great Debate, in H. Tomlinson (ed.) *Education and Training 14–19*. Harlow: Longman.

Laycock, T. (1996) Aunt Sally at the Woodhead show (letter), *Times Educational Supplement*, 15 March.

Mac an Ghaill, M. (1992a) Teachers' work: curriculum restructuring, culture, power and comprehensive schooling, *British Journal of Sociology of Education*, 13 (2), 179–99.

Mac an Ghaill, M. (1992b) Student perspectives on curriculum innovation and change in an English secondary school: an empirical study, *British Educational Research Journal*, 18 (3), 221–34.

Macfarlane, E. (1996) Sir Ron and the great however, *Times Educational Supplement*, 12 April, 15.

Mackenzie, R.F. (1970) *State School*. Harmondsworth: Penguin Books.

Mackinnon, D. (1996) What should we teach? Unit 1 in Block 3 of Open University EU208 course *Exploring Educational Issues*. Milton Keynes: Open University.

McKinnon, D., Nolan, P., Openshaw, R. and Soler, J. (1991) New Zealand curriculum innovation in historical and political context: the Freyberg integrated studies project and parallel projects of the 1940s, *Journal of Curriculum Studies*, 23 (2), 155–75.

Mackinnon, R. (1988) Developments in the curriculum and structures of upper secondary education in Australia: the last decade, *Journal of Curriculum Studies*, 20 (6), 493–508.

Magee, B. (1978) An introduction to philosophy: an interview with Isaiah Berlin, in *Men of Ideas*. London: BBC Publications.

Major, J. (1993) Speech to Conservative Party conference, October, and subsequent party political broadcast.

Mandelson, P. and Liddle, R. (1996) *The Blair Revolution*. London: Faber & Faber.

Marsh, C.J. (1994) *Introducing a National Curriculum: Plans and Paranoia*. New South Wales: Allen & Unwin.

Mayer, E. (1992) Employment-related competencies for post-compulsory education and training. A discussion paper, Mayer Committee, Melbourne.

Mazrui, A. (1980) *The African Condition: the Reith Lectures*. London: Heinemann.

Menter, I. and White, R. (eds) (1997) *Views from the West*. In preparation.

Moon, B. (1996) One foot in the past, *The Guardian*, 5 March.

Morrell, D. (1966) *Education and Change*. The Annual Joseph Payne Memorial Lectures 1965–6. London: College of Preceptors.

Morris, M. (1981) Banal lesson, *The Teacher*, 23 January, 3.

MSC (1981) *Using Residential Experience in YOP*. London: MSC.

Murdoch, E. and Dunning, J. (1993) Curriculum change in Scotland 1972–1992, in H. Tomlinson (ed.) *Education and Training 14–19*. Harlow: Longman.

Naish, M. and Rawlings, E. (1990) Geography 16–19: some implications for higher education, *Journal of Geography in Higher Education*, 14 (1).

National Commission on Education (1993) *Learning to Succeed*. London: Heinemann.

NFER (Stradling, R., Saunders, L. and Weston, P.) (1991) *Differentiation in Action: a Whole School Approach for Raising Attainment*. London: HMSO.

National Union of Teachers (1995a) *14–19 Strategy for the Future: the Road to Equality*. London: NUT.

National Union of Teachers (1995b) *Teachers' Views of 14–19 Education*. A pilot project involving NUT, Goldsmiths' College and London Institute of Education, available from NUT, Hamilton House, London.

Newby, M. (1996) Foggy day? Send in the philosophers (letter), *Times Educational Supplement*, 15 March.

Nielsen, H. (1991) Report on history teaching in secondary schools, paper presented at Council of Europe symposium, History Teaching in the New Europe, Bruges, December.

O'Connor, M. (1987) *Curriculum at the Crossroads*. An account of the SCDC national conference on aspects of curriculum change, University of Leeds, September.

OECD (1994) *Issues in Education in Asia and the Pacific*. Paris: OECD.

OECD (1995) *Education at a Glance*. Paris: OECD.

Okuya, T., Miyakawa, H., Hatano, Y. and Kadowaki, T. (1993) The new national curriculum of technology education in Japan, *The Technology Teacher*, November.

Ozga, J. (1989) *Teachers as a Workforce*. Open University E208 course Unit 19. Milton Keynes: Open University.

Parkes, Sir Edward (1990) Interview on Woman's Hour, BBC Radio 4, 28 March.

Paulter, A. (1993) The American experience, in H. Tomlinson (ed.) *Education and Training 14–19*. Harlow: Longman.

Peddiwell, J. (1939) *The Sabre Toothed Curriculum*. New York: McGraw-Hill.

Pilger, J. (1996) The Dunblanes that are never news, *New Statesmen and Society*, 5 April, 14–15.

Pollard, A. and Tann, S. (1993) *Reflective Teaching in the Primary School*. London: Cassell.

Porkess, K. (1995) *MEI Structured Mathematics, Five Years On*. Plymouth: University of Plymouth.

PRAISE (1987) *Interim Evaluation Report*. Bristol: Bristol University/Open University.

Pring, R. (1989) The curriculum and the new vocationalism, *British Journal of Education and Work*, 1 (3), 133–48.

Pring, R. (1995a) *Closing the Gap: Liberal Education and Vocational Preparation*. London: Hodder & Stoughton.

Pring, R. (1995b) Editorial, *British Journal of Educational Studies*, 42 (2).

Pring, R. (1996) Interview for *The Universities Award*. Bristol: ASDAN.

Pring, R., White, R. and Brockington, D. (1982) *The 14–18 Curriculum*. London: Schools Council.

Proctor, N. (1988) Government control of the curriculum: some archive and recent evidence, *British Educational Research Journal*, 14 (2), 155–65.

Pyke, N. (1996a) Heads set to wreck tables, *Times Educational Supplement*, 10 May, 1.

Pyke, N. (1996b) Welsh win praise from inspector, *Times Educational Supplement*, 23 February, 8.

Radford, T. (1996) Population growth feeds a world crisis, *The Guardian*, 13 April, 6.

Rafferty, F. (1996) English pupils years behind, *Times Educational Supplement*, 19 January, 1.

Reynolds, D. and Farrell, S. (1996) *World's Apart? Review of International Surveys of Educational Achievement Involving England*. London: Ofsted.

Rhoades, G. (1989) Conceptions and institutional categories of curriculum; cross national comparisons of upper secondary education, *Journal of Curriculum Studies*, 21 (1).

Richardson, W., Spours, K., Woolhouse, J. and Young, M. (1995) *Learning for the Future: Initial Report*. London University Institute of Education Post 16 Centre/Warwick University Centre for Education and Industry.

Rogers, C. (1983) *Freedom to Learn in the 1980s*. Columbus, OH: Charles Merrill.

Rutter, M. *et al.* (1979) *Fifteen Thousand Hours*. Wells: Open Books.

Ryle, S. and White, M. (1996) UK slips in world league, *The Guardian*, 28 May, 1.

Sanderson, M. (1983) *Education, Economic Change and Society in England 1780–1870*. London: Macmillan.

Schon, D. (1983) *The Reflective Teacher*. London: Temple Smith.

Schools Council (1973) *Evaluation in Curriculum Development: Twelve Case Studies*. London: Macmillan.

Schools Council (1981) *The Practical Curriculum*. London: Schools Council.

Scottish Office (1994) *Higher Still: Opportunity for All, Principles for the Post-16 Curriculum*: Edinburgh: HMSO.

Seckington, R. (1993) Key Stage 4, *Forum*, 35 (1), 11–13.

Secondary Heads Association (1994) *16–19 Pathways to Achievement*. London: SHA.

Seifert, R. (1987) *Teacher Militancy: a History of Teachers' Strikes 1896–1987*. Lewes: Falmer Press.

Skelton, A. (1990) Towards confinement and retreat: the changing face of curriculum integration in Sheffield 1986–90, *School Organisation*, 10 (2/3), 229–38.

Skilbeck, M. (1984) Curriculum evaluation at the national level, in M. Skilbeck (ed.) *Evaluating the Curriculum in the Eighties*. London: Hodder & Stoughton.

Smithers, A. (1993) *All Our Futures: Britain's Education Revolution*. Dispatches report for Channel 4, December.

Sofer, A. (1995) Free the butterfly from the strait-jacket, *Times Educational Supplement*, 2 June.

Steiner, R. (1971) *Human Values in Education*. New York: Rudolf Steiner Press.

Stenhouse, L. (1967) *Culture and Education*. London: Nelson.

Stenhouse, L. (1975) *An Introduction to Curriculum Research*. London: Nelson.

Task Group on Assessment and Testing (1988) *National Curriculum: a Report*. London: Department of Education and Science.

Taverner, R. (1996) Thousands tainted with the Woodhead syndrome (letter), *Times Educational Supplement*, 1 March.

Thames TV (1983) *Tales out of School*.

Thaning, K. (1982) *NFS Grundtvig*. Copenhagen: Det Danske Selskab.

Thodberg, C. and Thyssen, A. (1983) *NFS Grundtvig: Tradition and Renewal*. Copenhagen: Det Danske Selskab.

Thorne, M. (1987) The legacy of the Microelectronics Education Programme, *British Journal of Educational Technology*, 18 (3).

Tomlinson, H. (1993) *Education and Training 14–19: Continuity and Diversity in the Curriculum*. Harlow: Longman.

Tomlinson, S. (1995) Partnership should be a priority now, *Times Educational Supplement*, 1 September, 12.

Tropp, A. (1957) *The Schoolteachers: the Growth of the Teaching Profession in England and Wales from 1800 to the Present Day*. London: Heinemann.

Truman, P. (1985) Valediction or obituary? A critical assessment of the contribution of the Schools Council to curriculum development in this country, *Curriculum*, 6 (1): 10–16.

Tween, T. (1996) To compete we need to be able to compare like with like (letter), *Times Educational Supplement*, 29 April.

UCAS (1996) *Guide to Applicants* (Note 72K). Cheltenham: UCAS.

Walker, J. (1979) *Changing the Curriculum: the GYSL Experience*. Sheffield: Sheffield City Polytechnic.

Way, N. (1985) The TSW Youth Award Scheme, *NOISE Journal*, 4 (1), 5.

Weinstock, A. (1976) I blame the teachers, *Times Educational Supplement*, 23 January.

West, J. (1996) What about some praise for a change? (letter), *Times Educational Supplement*, 23 February.

Weston, P. and Stradling, R. (1993) Setting the 14–19 curriculum in a European perspective, in H. Tomlinson (ed.) *Education and Training 14–19*. Harlow: Longman.

White, R. (1980) *Absent with Cause*. London: Routledge & Kegan Paul.

White, R. (1994) The significance of the affective domain in the Danish system of education. BERA Conference Paper, Oxford.

White, R. and Brockington, D. (1978) *In and Out of School*. London: Routledge & Kegan Paul.

White, R. and Brockington, D. (1983) *Tales out of School: Consumers' Views of British Education*. London: Routledge & Kegan Paul.

White, R. and Drower, C. (1993) The European dimension as a determinant of student teacher classroom practice. BERA Conference Paper, Liverpool.

Whitehead, M. (1996) Professor urges new direction for research, *Times Educational Supplement*, 26 April.

Whitty, G. (1983) State policy and school examinations, in J. Ahier and M. Flude (eds) *Contemporary Education Policy*. London: Croom Helm.

Whitty, G. (1985) *Sociology and School Knowledge*. London: Methuen.

Wiener, M. (1985) *English Culture and the Decline of the Industrial Spirit 1850–1980*. Harmondsworth: Penguin.

Williams, R. (1961) *The Long Revolution*. Harmondsworth: Penguin.

Williams, R. and Yeomans, D. (1994) The Technical and Vocational Education Initiative and school autonomy in the management of curriculum change, *Research Papers in Education*, 9 (3), 303–19.

Woodhead, C. (1996) Chief Inspector's annual report, *Times Educational Supplement*, 9 February, 4.

Woods, P. (1995) Teaching. Open University EU208 course, *Exploring Educational Issues*, Unit 2. Milton Keynes: Open University.

Wragg, T. (1996) Put a fresh spin on all that tough talk, *Times Educational Supplement*, 22 March.

Young, M., Hodgson, A. and Leney, T. (1995) *Unifying the Post-compulsory Curriculum: Lessons from France to Scotland*. London: Institute of Education, University of London.

Young, M. and Whitty, G. (1977) *Society, State and Schooling*. Lewes: Falmer.

Index

ENCOURAGING LEARNING
TOWARDS A THEORY OF THE LEARNING SCHOOL

Jon Nixon, Jane Martin, Penny McKeown and Stewart Ranson

This book offers a radical critique of both the Government's agenda for educational reform and of the various alternative agendas that have been proposed in recent years. It is based upon original research by a distinguished inter-disciplinary author team.

The focus of the book is on the work of secondary schools located in contexts of disadvantage and on the overwhelming need to motivate young people and to foster in them a sense of purpose and optimism for the future.

In particular, the authors discuss:

- how broader social trends impact upon schools as they move towards the year 2000;
- ways of understanding the low educational expectations of many young people and their disaffected attitude towards schooling;
- strategies by which schools can motivate students to take responsibility for their own learning;
- ways of working in partnership with parents and in collaboration with other schools.

The book is based on the premise that if schools in contexts of disadvantage can be made to work, then schools in other more favourable contexts will have much to learn from them. The book will be of interest to teachers and headteachers, educational policy makers and social scientists with a professional interest in educational and management issues.

Contents

Preface – The limits of the present reform agendas – Towards a theory of learning – The learning school I – The learning school II – Towards the twenty-first century – References – Index.

160pp   0 335 19087 1 (Paperback)   0 335 19088 X (Hardback)

STUDYING CURRICULUM
CASES AND METHODS

Ivor F. Goodson

Studying Curriculum offers a fruitful and practical approach for analysing the inescapable political realities of the contemporary curriculum. It reminds us that what is socially constructed can also be deconstructed and reconstructed, and that notions of social equity and justice can be reconstituted within school curricula. As Andy Hargreaves notes in his critical introduction to this volume: 'such a combination of conceptual and political radicalism, and empirical and historical realism not only defines Goodson's scholarship but also demystifies the curriculum it addresses'.

Ivor Goodson explores how and by whom the curriculum is controlled. He examines how social background and origin, historical and political context, and school curriculum are interrelated. He takes a social constructionist approach, and plants this firmly in the 'middle ground' of subjects – their traditions, departments and politics. This enables both a rendering of the experience of those working within these traditions; and a reaching outwards to the structures and assumptions underlying those subject traditions.

Contents

160pp   0 335 19050 2 (Paperback)   0 335 19051 0 (Hardback)

EDUCATION AND THE STRUGGLE FOR DEMOCRACY
THE POLITICS OF EDUCATIONAL IDEAS

Wilfred Carr and Anthony Hartnett

During the past decade there has been a series of radical changes to the educational system of England and Wales. This book argues that any serious study of these changes has to engage with complex questions about the role of education in a modern liberal democracy. Were these educational changes informed by the needs and aspirations of a democratic society? To what extent will they promote democratic values and ideals? These questions can only be adequately addressed by making explicit the political ideas and the underlying philosophical principles that have together shaped the English educational system. To this end, the book provides a selective history of English education which exposes the connections between decisive periods of educational change and the intellectual and political climate in which it occurred. It also connects the educational policies of the 1980s and 1990s to the political ideas of the New Right in order to show how they are part of a broader political strategy aimed at reversing the democratic advances achieved through the intellectual and political struggles of the nineteenth and twentieth centuries. The book proposes that a democratic educational vision can only effectively be advanced by renewing the 'struggle for democracy' – the historical struggle to create forms of education which will empower all citizens to participate in an open, pluralistic and democratic society.

Contents

256pp   0 335 19520 2 (Paperback)   0 335 19521 0 (Hardback)